Meditation, Writing Can Help You Attain

ENLIGHTENMENT

PANKAJ KUMAR

ISBN 979-8-89133-445-8

Contents

Acknowledgements 7

1. The Path Shown By Two Great Men **9**

The life and teachings of Swami Sivananada—Spiritual lessons from a saint-politician—Life and teachings of Mahatma Gandhi—George Orwell on Gandhi

2. Glimpses of Religions, Religious Philosophies and Marxism **17**

How Anil gained from his association with the Brahma Kumaris—Life of the Buddha—The basics of Buddhism—A wonderful ancient religious philosophy, Jainism—Aspects of Islam—Hare Krishna practices—Some aspects of Marxism

3. The Gita and the Sermon on the Mount **31**

Meditating on the Gita for strength, guidance—The Gita gives us hope, courage—The Sermon on the Mount in commandments—Do not resist an evil person—Intuition and the inner voice

4. On Writing and Reading **39**

Khushwant Singh on writing—Luann Budd on journal writing—Julia Cameron on journal writing and creativity—Great suggestions from Anne Lamott—Lessons from Premchand's short story 'The Writer'—Excessive reading can make us feel dull—Characteristics of a good inspirational book—On editing a writeup

5. The Simple Spiritual Practices of Japa, Pranayama..53

Japa, a suitable practice for householders—Evolution of Anil's japa practice—Mahatma Gandhi on Ramanama—Pranayama and meditation apps

6. On Staying Physically Healthy.........................61

Suggestions for good health from Mahatma Gandhi—The gift of good health—On avoiding gluttony—Psychological benefits of walking—How Anil gave up tobacco addiction

7. Staying at the Peak of Our Mental Powers.........71

On staying mentally fit—Some basic books on psychology—Philippa Perry on mental health—Thomas Szasz on mental illness—Dr Sudhir Kakar on psychotherapy—The contribution of Sigmund Freud—On client-centred therapy—Viktor Frankl on having a meaningful life—Understanding schizophrenia—Dale Carnegie's self-help book

8. Understanding How Journalists Work 83

The news story and gathering news—The experience of reporting—What Rohit learnt at a students' newspaper—On reading the news

9. Worldly Success, Spiritual Evolution and the Life of Our Dreams 93

Worldly success as well as spiritual growth—The best practices of Pranab Mukherjee—On daily routines—Our contribution to society and an adequate income—Rohit's simple philosophy of work—On managing work

10. The Well-being of Spouse and Children 101

Suggestions for a spiritually inclined couple—A devoted wife—The education of our children—Gandhi on the education of children—Study tips by B Stevenson—A scheme for self-education of youngsters—For better conversations—Listening can revive relationships

11. The Wisdom of Tolstoy, Gibran, Khushwant Singh, Dr Chopra, Krishnamurti.................... 113

Should Anil become a monk?—The intuitive wisdom of Kahlil Gibran—Views of Khushwant Singh on religion—Dr Deepak Chopra on finding joy in life—Krishnamurti on knowledge and education

12. Restful Sleep and Working All Night............. 123

How to get restful sleep—Sleep and spiritual practices

13. The Control and Sublimation of Desire.......... 129

Controlling desire enables us to achieve lofty goals—Celibacy for householders over 40 years of age—Avoiding heavy meals at night

14. Keep on Trying, Live in the Present, Surrender to God's Will 135

The importance of trying—The concept of surrender—When everything seems uncertain—Living one day at a time—Coping with evil in the world—When major worldly problems arise

Acknowledgements

First of all, I would like to thank my family: My parents late Dr Pashupati Nath Singh and Mrs Prabhabati Singh for giving me a good education; my wife Shyama Singh for support and encouragement for 30 years; my son Aishwarya Pranjal for giving me hope and cheerfulness; and my siblings Navin and Shashi for their goodwill.

I am deeply grateful to the writers who inspire me each time I read them. Swami Sivananda's books are my intellectual gurus. From time to time, I draw strength and inspiration from the works of Christmas Humphreys, Mahatma Gandhi, VS Naipaul, George Orwell, RK Narayan, Khushwant Singh, Robin Sharma, Dr Deepak Chopra, Swami Prabhupada, Dr Janette Rainwater, Dr Sudhir Kakar, Anne Lamott, Luann Budd, Sankarshan Das Adhikari (who offers an ISKCON e-course), Thubten Chodron, Will Durant, and several other writers.

I am thankful to the saints late Guruma Alkeshwari Devi, Shri Shambhu Prasad Sati, the Brahma Kumaris, and Shri Binod Kumar for guidance.

Numerous people have helped me, but in particular I would like to mention John Stephen Veitch from New Zealand for guidance on journal writing, Upala Sen for help and advice related to my career, and PP Wangchuk for advice.

Finally, I am thankful to the organizations that have given me employment during the past 30 years.

1.

The Path Shown By Two Great Men

The life and teachings of Swami Sivananada—Spiritual lessons from a saint-politician—Life and teachings of Mahatma Gandhi—George Orwell on Gandhi

1.a.The life and teachings of Swami Sivananada

Swami Sivananda (1887-1963) was a doctor who had renounced the world and shone as a yogi. Living in a hut in Rishikesh, Uttarakhand, he wrote several hundred books and also founded the Divine Life Society.

Two of his books which I like to read again and again are 'Sure Ways for Success in Life and God-realisation' and 'Japa Yoga'. I also like to reread his autobiography, and books on brahmacharya, sound sleep and self-knowledge.

I give here some of his teachings which contain the best elements of different religions that he had found beneficial from his own experiences. But he emphasised more on the Vedanta philosophy of Hinduism.

He said we can do japa (repetition of mantras or chanting) for one or two hours daily. We can try to achieve the ideal of brahmacharya (freedom from sexual thoughts and desires). Keeping a diary is a great help in the spiritual path. It is better to become a vegetarian and give up smoking and drinking. Going for walks or doing yoga asanas will keep us healthy, he said.

He said desire and anger impel man to commit sin, so we must try to control them. We should try not to speak harsh words to anyone. If someone abuses us or calls us names, we can try to remain silent. This is the spiritual practice of ahimsa, he said.

We can avoid watching movies which are full of sex and violence as they fill our minds with base thoughts.

The attraction to wealth and women keeps us rooted in this world. We can strive to become brahmacharis. After checking passion, we will enjoy peace from within.

A sincere attempt is all that God expects from us. We can do our best and leave the results in His hands.

Idle talk is a waste of our mental energy, he said. We must try to observe mauna (silence) for one or two hours daily. Indulging in gossip will distract our mind and make it difficult to meditate or read something serious.

We can follow the teachings of religion, keep on trying, and surrender to the will of God. God will do what is good for us.

We should try to do some work regularly without too much concern about the rewards. We also need to fulfil our duties towards our family members. It is important to educate our children and teach them the basics so that they can survive.

He said some people waste their time in gossiping, smoking and drinking, watching inane TV programmes and pointless movies. Some other people visit prostitutes. Instead of these activities, one can do spiritual sadhana, read good books and do physical exercises in one's free time.

The Divine Life Society founded by him has done excellent work in spreading his teachings worldwide. The organisation has published his books and spread his message across the world.

1. b. Spiritual lessons from a saint-politician

We can learn several spiritual lessons from Mohandas Karamchand Gandhi (1869 to 1948), who was a saintly man and also a leader of the Indian freedom movement. He was non-sectarian and accepted what was the best in different religions.

Gandhi derived his spiritual strength from repeating Ramanama and regular reading of chapter 2 of the Gita. He imposed several disciplines on himself: He repeated the name of God and avoided meat, alcohol, tobacco and sex. He went for a walk daily and also wrote books and articles for newspapers.

He did not do yoga asanas or pranayama but did japa or mantra meditation. As a child when he was afraid of ghosts, a nurse advised him to repeat the name of God. He began the practice which became a source of strength during his struggles later in life. He said one could repeat Ramanama when one gets worried or while doing brain work or even during pauses in conversation.

In his late thirties he took the vow of brahmacharya or celibacy. He said, "The conquest of lust is the highest endeavour of a man or woman's existence." He believed that Ramanama combined with brahmacharya (celibacy) could cure mental and psychosomatic ailments.

He observed a vow of silence at certain times and said, "Silence is part of the spiritual discipline of a votary of truth."

Gandhi writes in his autobiography that he was influenced by his conversations with Raychandbhai, who was in the gem business but was essentially a spiritual man. He kept a diary and a spiritual book on his study table at office. Whenever Raychandbhai was free, he would read the book or write in his diary. All his published writings were extracts from this diary. Whenever he got a chance, he would engage Gandhi in a conversation on spiritual subjects. But despite his attainments, Gandhi could not enthrone Raychandbhai in his heart as his guru. The Guru's place remained vacant in Gandhi's heart.

In difficult situations something from within tells us what we should do or not do which it called intuition, the inner voice or our conscience. This is different from reasoning or arriving at conclusions by thinking, the Mahatma said.

Gandhi sometimes heard this voice which enabled him to take major decisions. He says one should not disbelieve that an inner voice exists. But you need to purify your mind if you want to hear this voice clearly.

He was in favour of a vegetarian diet that included milk. He felt that ideally, food should be taken like medicine to stay healthy and not just to satisfy the taste buds. One can fast once a fortnight. You can have one meal in the day and have fruits at other times. Fasting from time to time gives rest to the digestive system and improves health. You can concentrate more easily on meditation. Fasting also helps you to control the desire for sensual enjoyments. It helps not only in controlling gluttony but also in observing brahmacharya. We can concentrate easily on prayer if we do it on an empty stomach.

The Gita says we should eat neither too little nor too much. The emphasis is on alpahar or meagreness of food. Gandhi says that mortification of the flesh is necessary when the flesh is not under the control of the mind, but when it is already under control, then fasting is not necessary. Gluttony is a common weakness of man which we can bring under control by periodical fasting.

Gandhi's views on material poverty are interesting but controversial. He said that possession of material things implies provision for the future. A spiritual person should try to live in the present and not worry too much about the future. A spiritual aspirant should ask God to provide his daily bread (which means all the essential things he needs for himself and his loved ones). He does not ask for tomorrow's bread. The earth has enough resources for the needs of humans. The problem arises because some people try to hoard resources as a result of which many others go hungry.

1. c. Life and teachings of Mahatma Gandhi

Spiritual leader and social activist Gandhi has inspired millions across the world.

He was a religious man who wrote about religion and tried to practise what he preached. As a political leader, he spread awareness about the freedom struggle among the masses.

Bharatan Kumarappa has compiled and edited Gandhi's writings on religion in his book 'My Religion'. Gandhi had read about all the major religions and followed what he intuitively felt was the best in each. He was not sectarian or communal in any way.

His ideas on health are given in the booklet 'Key to Health'. It has chapters on food, alcohol, tobacco and brahmacharya.

He was in favour of a vegetarian diet. One can have two or three meals a day with plenty of fruits and vegetables. He did not find merit in the argument that moderate drinking was good for health. And he agreed with Leo Tolstoy that tobacco was the worst intoxicant because it was the most convenient. He said tea and coffee are not required by the body, so we should cut down on their consumption.

He felt that even married couples should try to observe brahmacharya after the first few years of marriage. Brahmacharya is a great help in the spiritual path.

He did not like the existing system of education. He had his own ideas on education, but some of his own children had complaints that he did provide them a regular education.

If we want ideas for the education of our children, we can read the chapters on the education of children in his autobiography 'The Story of My Experiments with Truth'. There are four chapters which can be read in about half an hour.

Many modern writers on Gandhi discuss mainly his life and thoughts as a political activist but ignore his views on religion.

His goal was the Hindu ideal of self-realisation or meeting God face to face.

1. d. George Orwell on Gandhi

I have great respect for both Orwell and Gandhi, so I read Orwell's views on Gandhi with interest. In his essay 'Reflections on Gandhi,' Orwell said that though he did not feel much admiration for Gandhi because of his other worldly outlook, he did not think that the Indian leader was a failure. Gandhi was a capable man who could have succeeded in many fields. The main objective for which he had worked for—the independence of India—had been achieved.

Orwell said as Gandhi's aims were other worldly, he tried to ensure spiritual growth instead of improving the condition of humankind on earth. So, Gandhi could not be called a humanist, felt Orwell.

Orwell said that it is possible that Gandhi was driven by vanity. He thought of himself as someone sitting on a prayer mat and moving empires.

Gandhi imposed certain disciplines on himself which one can try to follow to some extent: He avoided meat, alcohol, tobacco and sex. He also felt that food should be taken as medicine to maintain health and not for enjoyment. Meat, alcohol, tobacco and sex are things a saint should avoid, but sainthood is something humans should try to avoid, according to Orwell.

Both Gandhi and Orwell were great men: Gandhi was a great spiritual leader and activist while Orwell was a great thinker and writer. We can ponder over the writings of these two men and accept the things that appeal to us.

* * * * *

2.

Glimpses of Religions, Religious Philosophies and Marxism

How Anil gained from his association with the Brahma Kumaris—Life of the Buddha—The basics of Buddhism—A wonderful ancient religious philosophy, Jainism—Some aspects of Islam—Hare Krishna practices—Some aspects of Marxism

2. a. How Anil gained from his association with the Brahma Kumaris

The Prajapita Brahma Kumari Ishwariya Vishvidyalaya is a spiritual organisation founded by Brahma Baba (Dada Lekh Raj Kripalani) in Western India in the 1930s. The organisation has grown steadily since then and has followers in many parts of the world. The headquarters are in Mount Abu, Rajasthan.

Followers can stay with their families and continue in their jobs, but they should try to give up five evils: Lust, anger, greed, attachment, pride.

Even married devotees try to be celibate. Followers take a vegetarian diet which includes milk. Tea in moderation is permitted. It is better if the food is cooked by a devotee.

Devotees listen to the murli (sermon) in the morning or evening and sit in meditation before an image of Brahma Baba or Lord Shiva in a quiet room or hall. They avoid movies, television and to some extent, newspapers and news sites. They lay more emphasis on spiritual growth rather than physical exercises.

One of the teachings is that time is cyclical and repeats itself after several thousand years. It is said that what is happening now had happened earlier. This philosophy helps one to accept misfortune and good luck with equanimity and a cool mind, but one should keep on making an effort (do purusharth). One can grow spiritually only by striving hard.

On special occasions there is all day meditation, one sitting in the morning and the next sometime after lunch. A spiritually advanced devotee sits on a platform and meditates facing the other meditators who look at his or her forehead. One keeps one's eyes open or half open during the meditation. Tea can be had if one feels drowsy.

Anil was fortunate to have come in contact with the Brahma Kumaris. He got a sense of direction early in life. Even though he was not able to keep up the contact, he gained immensely from his association with them in his youth. There have been changes in the organisation since that time. As a young man he was troubled by worldly ambitions and physical desires which were calmed down and he got a sense of purpose and direction in life because of his association with them.

2. b. Life of the Buddha

When Siddhartha was born, astrologers prophesied that he would become either a great king or a great spiritual leader. His father wanted him to become an emperor, so the king kept him protected from suffering in his childhood and adolescence. Siddhartha got married to Yashodhara at the age of 16, and they had a son, Rahul.

As he grew older, he wanted to explore the world and one day asked his charioteer to take him on a ride of the city. He went out on four rides and saw four different sights. He first saw an old man, then a sick man, then a dead man and finally he saw a hermit. He asked his charioteer who they were and what had happened to them. The charioteer explained that old age, illness, and death happen to everyone. The last man was a hermit who had renounced sensual pleasures in search of wisdom.

The four sights made him think and he decided to leave the palace to search for the truth. It was night. He had one last look at his sleeping wife and child and left the palace to find the way to end suffering for himself and others.

He went to the sages Uddaka and Alara Kalama but their teachings did not satisfy him fully. He resolved to search for the truth by his own efforts.

He practised austerities, renounced sensual pleasures and meditated for six years. Eventually, he realised that truth could not be found in austerities and decided to adopt a middle path between asceticism and sensuality. He began to eat moderately and regained his strength.

Meditating under a tree, he attained enlightenment on a full moon night in May. He had compassion for suffering humankind and decided to teach people the way to end suffering.

He spent the rest of his life in teaching the way to end suffering and attain enlightenment. Some people became lay disciples and others became monks to join the order founded by him. When he visited his palace, his son asked him for his inheritance. He asked the monks to admit his son to the order. His wife too became a nun.

He spent many years teaching and passed away at a ripe old age.

2. c. The basics of Buddhism

To understand the basics of Buddhism, you need to know about the life of the Buddha, the Four Noble Truths, the Noble Eightfold Path and the law of karma.

The highest being in Buddhism is the arhat. In an arhat the base desires have died out and he or she does not experience suffering. Buddhism also mentions the concept of Bodhisattva. A Bodhisatva is one who has delayed his or her own enlightenment and taken birth in order to help suffering people.

The law of karma is a basic concept in Hinduism, Buddhism and Jainism. Scientists say the natural world such as the Sun, moon, and planets move according to laws. In the same way human affairs are governed by laws. One is rewarded for good thoughts, words and deeds and punished for bad ones. This is done by the Universe and one need not think of a God who dispenses rewards and punishments.

The Four Noble Truths are basic to Buddhism: 1. There is widespread suffering in the world; 2. Selfish or evil desire is the cause of suffering; 3. Elimination of desire eliminates suffering; 4. Desire can be eliminated by walking on the Noble Eightfold Path.

The Noble Eightfold Path is the most important part of Buddhism. It consists of 1. Right Views: You need to know the basics of Buddhist philosophy. 2. Right motives: You should have noble aims, that is, you should try to achieve your own enlightenment and help others attain it. 3. Right Speech: You should avoid telling lies, idle talk, and speaking harsh words. 4. Right action: You should try to abstain from killing, stealing, unwise sexual behaviour, lying and intoxicants (These are known as the Panchashil or Five Precepts). 5. Right livelihood: You should take up a trade of occupation that is compatible with religion. 6. Right effort: You need to keep on trying. 7. Right concentration and 8. Right meditation: This will ensure your rapid mental and spiritual evolution. Buddhism lays stress on breathing meditation and repetition of mantras.

When you are mentally prepared, you can decide to follow the Five Precepts of Buddhism. The promise is made to oneself and not to some external being.

Advanced practitioners decide to follow the Eight Precepts. You may follow the Eight Precepts for a day or a fortnight or a longer period. In the beginning you may not be able to follow the Five Precepts fully but as you advance on the spiritual path, you will be able to do so to a greater extent.

The additional three precepts are as follows: 1. Abandon singing, dancing, playing music, wearing ornaments, perfumes and cosmetics; 2. Avoid sitting on a high or expensive seat or bed; 3. Avoid eating after midday. The last precept may be tough for many people. If you cannot follow it, try to avoid rich, heavy food at night. You can sometimes have just fruits for dinner.

Even if you do not call yourself a Buddhist or you are an atheist, you can benefit by trying to follow the Five Precepts or the Panchashil. You can also read basic books on Buddhism on holidays.

2. d. A wonderful ancient religious philosophy, Jainism

The word Jain comes from Jina or conqueror, one who has conquered the worldly passions of lust, anger, greed and pride by his own efforts. Conquest of oneself is a greater achievement than conquest of nations.

Lord Mahavira was an enlightened soul who systematised and reformed Jainism which had been founded earlier. He was born in a royal family in a town near Patna in Bihar in 599 BC. He was reared in the lap of luxury but at the age of about 30, he renounced the world, practised austerities, meditated and attained the highest state of knowledge. He then travelled from place to place. At the age of 72, he cut off the ties of birth, old age and death.

Lord Mahavira said one could attain the highest state by practising the Tri-ratna or the three jewels: right faith, right knowledge and right conduct. Right conduct means we should abstain from violence, theft, sensuality, and should be truthful and not accumulate wealth (this precept is intended for monks).

The law of ahimsa or non-violence has an important place in Jainism. "Ahimsa paramo dharma" or non-violence is the highest religion. We should try not to hurt any living being.

Like Hindus and Buddhists, Jains also believe in the law of karma. It means that the universe rewards you for good deeds and punishes you for evil ones. You can dissolve evil karma of the past by spiritual practices such as meditation.

Unlike the followers of several major religions, Jains do not believe in a personal God. The highest being in Jainism is an enlightened human being and not a God. He or she has conquered the lower nature, acquired knowledge, does no evil while living and does not take birth again. After death, his or her soul merges in the infinite.

According to Jain philosophy, the universe has always existed. We can classify all things into two categories: matter and soul. Everything in the universe functions according to laws and not according to the wishes of a

God. Only enlightened human beings fully understand these laws. Jains believe in God and consider Him as omniscient and omnipotent but do not consider him as the creator of the Universe. They lay great stress on morality and say that one who is free from lust, anger, greed and pride is enlightened.

2. e. Some aspects of Islam

Islam is the name given to the religion founded by Prophet Muhammad who was born in Mecca, Arabia, in the year 570 AD. Here are some glimpses from Islam which means "submission to the will of God."

At one time the Prophet used to graze cattle. He liked to retire into a cave and once the Angel Gabriel came to him and asked him to recite. The teachings of Islam were revealed to the Prophet over several days in this manner.

When the Prophet told his wife about the experience, she recognized him as the Nabi or Prophet.

The most important teachings are the five pillars of Islam: 1. Iman or creed: Muslims believe that there is no God save Allah and Prophet Muhammad is his messenger. 2. Offer Namaz or prayer regularly. 3. Zakat. Muslims are exhorted to donate a part of their income regularly to the less fortunate. 4. Fasting: Muslims fast during the holy month of Ramadan. 5. Haj: The pilgrimage to Mecca is compulsory only for those who have the means.

These are the main teachings. Islam also stresses on avoiding gambling, adultery and other social evils. The holy book is the Quran. Abdullah Yusuf Ali has done an excellent translation of the holy book into English. Islam lays stress on reading the Quran regularly and also performing Dhikr or Zikr, which means the repetition of the word Allah or short phrases from the Quran. Muslims use a rosary called a tasbih or their fingers for counting the number of Dhikr.

Several Islamic scholars have said that the term jihad or holy war refers mainly to fighting against the evil inside oneself and not waging war against unbelievers.

Islam does not advise asceticism. A Muslim is expected to lead a holy life while living in this world. But a sect in Islam, the Sufis, do practice austerities. For spiritual renewal from time to time, they stay in seclusion, eat less, talk less, perform Dhikr and read the Quran. Sufis perform Dhikr in a group also. When one gets some free time, Dhikr is an excellent practice for Muslims to regain their spiritual strength and enthusiasm.

2. f. Hare Krishna practices

Members of the International Society of Krishna Consciousness (ISKCON), known as Hare Krishnas, follow certain spiritual disciplines which all aspirants can try to do to a certain extent for spiritual growth. Swami Prabhupada had founded the spiritual movement.

Devotees give up four things: Illicit sex, intoxicants, meat, and gambling. They read the Bhagavad Gita regularly and repeat the Hare Krishna mantra daily. After following these guidelines, they leave the rest in God's hands, that is, do total surrender to the Lord. When they face worldly problems, they do what they can and leave the rest to God.

For Hare Krishnas, sex is for procreation and not for recreation. They are advised to have sex only with their spouse and that too only for the purpose of having spiritually inclined children.

Hare Krishnas avoid all intoxicants, including tea, coffee, tobacco, alcohol, drugs. Some other Hindu spiritual organisations allow tea and coffee.

Devotees avoid meat, fish and eggs, but have milk. Some devotees also try to give up onion and garlic. Hare Krishnas do not indulge in gambling.

Advanced devotees do 16 rounds of the Hare Krishna mantra daily. The mantra is as follows: Hare Krishna, Hare Krishna, Krishna Krishna, Hare Hare/ Hare Rama, Hare Rama, Rama Rama, Hare Hare. They use a maala or rosary of 108 beads. The central bead is slightly bigger than the rest and is not counted. Each time they repeat the mantra, they move one bead ahead.

Devotees try to read the 'Bhagavad Gita As It Is' (which is a translation of the Sanskrit verses into Hindi and English) for some time daily depending on how much free time they have.

The disciplines seem to be strict. In the beginning one can follow them to the extent which one can do easily. As one advances on the spiritual path, one can follow them to a greater extent.

2. g. Some aspects of Marxism

We can briefly discuss some aspects of the philosophy of German philosopher Karl Marx (1818 to 1883), who was a major critic of religious philosophy and felt that religion was the opium of the masses that enabled them to forget their problems.

Marx, who was a social scientist and activist, said that production relations in a society (how goods and services are produced in a society) determine the superstructure (aspects of society such as culture, dress, means of entertainment). In other words, he felt that economic factors determine other factors in society.

He used to visit the British Museum Library in London regularly the way people attend office. He studied social sciences, history and literature, and several other subjects for many years. He said that till now philosophers have only interpreted the world, but the point is to change it. His main works are The Communist Manifesto and several volumes of Das Kapital.

He wanted to create a socialist society where each individual would get what he needs and would contribute what he was capable of. He said that in a capitalist society the means of production were concentrated in a few hands while the masses could not fulfil their basic needs.

He said that the history of all societies was the history of class struggles. In a capitalist society there was a conflict between the capitalists or the wealthy and the workers. He advocated an overthrow of the ruling class and establishing a dictatorship of the proletariat or the workers.

Most philosophers feel that the use of violence to bring about a communist society would be counter-productive. The new rulers would become as oppressive as the ones they overthrew. George Orwell's novel 'Animal Farm' deals with this subject. In the novel, pigs overthrow the men who own an animal farm. After assuming power, the pigs become dictatorial and oppress the other animals. The novel was a fable that attacked Joseph Stalin's communist rule in Russia.

Mahatma Gandhi too advocated socialism but he felt that socialism should not be brought about by violence. He said that in a capitalist society, the wealthy should consider themselves to be trustees of their wealth and use their money for the welfare of the masses.

A practical problem which arises when the means of production (land, factories) are owned collectively by the government is that the workers lose the incentive to work hard. The output goes down. This was the experience in Soviet Russia when farms were taken over by the government. The peasants lost the incentive to work hard on the government-owned farms.

Marx said that the "ruling ideology was the ideology of the ruling class." In other words, the dominant views in a society would be the ideas of the ruling class.

Influenced by communist ideas, governments in many parts of the world have brought about reforms to counter the problems of a capitalist society such as laws to prevent monopolies and provide better working conditions for the employees. These have come about without the need for violent revolution. If violence was used, the new system would be as oppressive as the old one.

* * * * *

3.

The Gita and the Sermon on the Mount

Meditating on the Gita for strength, guidance—The Gita gives us hope, courage—The Sermon on the Mount in commandments—Do not resist an evil person—Intuition and the inner voice

3. a. Meditating on the Gita for strength, guidance

At times when we feel lost, directionless, and anxious, it can be a help to read the paraphrases of a few Gita shlokas to get inner strength and guidance.

Given here are some shlokas that Anil reads when he is sad and anxious. They help him to face his problems one step at a time. Some excellent translations of the Bhagawad Gita are by Swami Prabhupada published in Hindi and English by ISKCON, by Swami Sivananda in English, and the one published by Gita Press. If you do not know Sanskrit in which the original Gita was originally written, you can read the paraphrases in English, Hindi or other languages. If you wish to go further, you can read the commentaries by experts on each shloka.

The first shloka paraphrase that Anil reads is chapter 8, verse 14: Lord Krishna says that He is easily accessible by anyone who remembers Him constantly. If we want to find God, we should remember Him often. We can do japa or mantra meditation for some time every morning and then whenever we are free.

The next shloka Anil reads is 18.62. Lord Krishna tells His devotees to do total surrender to the Lord. This means that we should do what we can and leave the many things which are beyond our control in the hands of God. God will do what is good for us. We should follow the essential teachings of our religion and leave the rest to God.

Shloka 3.39 says that lust can cloud our pure consciousness and is our constant enemy. It means that lustful thoughts and desires can affect our powers of thinking, reasoning and understanding. It is difficult to eliminate desire from our mind totally, but we should try.

Shloka 2.47 is about our work and duties. We have a right to do our work or perform our duties, but this does not automatically entitle us to the fruits of our efforts. This means that we should do our work sincerely and not think too much about the rewards.

The above four are Anil's favourite shlokas. You would have your own favourites. You could read the entire Gita over a few Sundays or whenever you have a few days off. It is helpful to underline those verses that appeal to you. Later when you are depressed and anxious, you can read just these paraphrases.

If time is limited, you could read just chapter 2, which contains a summary of the entire Gita. If you want to go further, you can also read chapter 3 which is about work.

3. b. The Gita gives us hope, courage

Reading a few verses of the Gita, or the Sermon on the Mount in the Bible, or about the Noble Eightfold Path in Buddhism will give us strength and guidance to face challenges in life.

Lord Krishna says in the Gita: "Fixing your Mind on Me, you shall overcome every obstacle by My Grace." This means that we should remember God, make a sincere effort and leave the rest in His hands.

How can we find peace of mind in difficult times? When a man gives up desires of the mind and finds satisfaction from within, he is said to be a sthithaprajna or a man of steady wisdom. If we give up the desire for sensual pleasures, and meditate, pray or work, we will find peace from within.

The Lord says: "I am easily attainable by that ever-steadfast yogi who constantly remembers Me." Remembering God or japa is an easy way to attain God.

A man is noble if he gives up sensual pleasures and tries to do some work. We need to perform our duty without excessive concern about the reward. This is called nishkama karma. While doing our work we should not think too much about success or failure. During an economic crisis in the country, unemployed people can try to take up whatever work is available without excessive concern about the remuneration.

How should we meditate? We have to find a clean spot, sit erect, take a vow of brahmacharya (freedom from sexual thoughts and desires) and have God as the supreme goal. We can do japa or pranayama in this posture. But we need not go to extremes. "Yoga is not for him who eats too much or too little, or sleeps too much or too little." We have to exercise moderation in eating and sleeping. There is no need to practise severe austerities.

In this world when righteousness declines and unrighteousness become powerful, God takes birth. He destroys evil and establishes righteousness, says the Gita.

Lord Krishna says that there are three paths to salvation: Gyan marga or the path of knowledge, karma marga or the path of work, and bhakti marga or the path of devotion. We have to select one according to our temperament and life situation.

Death is in the hands of God and after that we are reborn. This process is similar to a man shedding old clothes and putting on new ones. The cycle of birth and death ends when a person attains mukti or liberation.

3. c. The Sermon on the Mount in commandments

Russian writer Leo Tolstoy has summarised the teachings of Lord Jesus in the Sermon on the Mount in five commandments. When we face worldly problems, we should focus on keeping the commandments and leave the rest in the hands of the Lord. They are as follows:

"Do not be angry at anyone." But if you do get angry, go and make up with the person. We should try not to bear animosity towards anyone.

"Do not philander." Adultery is wrong. We should have brahmacharya or celibacy as our ideal and for achieving it we need God's grace.

"Do not make oaths." We should say yes when we mean yes and no when we mean no.

"Do not oppose evil." When someone insults, abuses or criticises us, we should try to stay silent or give a brief explanation. We should try not to judge the person.

The last commandment mentioned by Tolstoy is as follows: "Do not differentiate between your homeland and that of others." All humans are the children of one God and hence they are brothers and sisters.

Tolstoy was not only a novelist, but also a religious philosopher. During the second half of his life, he began to live in accordance with the teachings of Christianity, particularly the Sermon on the Mount. He combined the four Gospels of the Bible into one narrative in his book The Gospel in Brief. In this book he devotes a chapter to the Sermon on the Mount which he has summarised in five commandments. These commandments can guide us in difficult times. In the book he left out things which he thought were unnecessary.

He says we should live in the present day. We should worry about being within the father's will (keeping the commandments) and leave the rest to God. There is no need to worry about what we shall eat, drink or wear tomorrow as God knows we need these things and will provide them.

He says we should beware of false prophets. They teach us to go against God's will. For instance, they teach violence and punishment.

3. d. Do not resist an evil person

The Bible tells us to "resist not evil." When people insult us or criticise us unfairly, we can stay silent. God will protect our interests. If possible, we can go further and try not to hate the person who has insulted us. Swami Sivananda says we can say mentally, "He is a baby soul. So, he has done it. Let me forgive him this time."

These five commandments can be compared with the Five Precepts of Buddhism or the Panchashil: Do not kill, steal, indulge in sensuality, tell lies or take intoxicants. Tolstoy does not include "do not steal" and "do not take intoxicants" in his list. He has also not stressed on the need to keep on trying and meditating regularly that are emphasised by the Noble Eightfold Path of Buddhism.

People in positions of power are sometimes aggressive and extrovert. They sometimes criticise others without a proper analysis.

We can stay silent when people in authority criticise us or our work. If necessary, we can give a brief explanation.

We can tell ourselves that God will protect our interests. Whatever is God's will will happen.

When people in authority ask us to do something which is unfair and difficult, we can try to do it but say mentally, "God does everything for my own good. Let Thy will be done."

If we sense an argument developing, we can stay silent. An argument will not solve the problem and will generate ill will.

While it may be necessary to obey people in authority, we may not necessarily respect them. They are not saints or intellectuals.

When strangers try to do something wrong, we have to protect ourselves or our interests. But there is no need to try to punish them.

3. e. Intuition and the inner voice

Intuition is the realisation of truth without hard thinking or perception through the senses. You feel from within that this is how it is, but you may not be able to express it clearly in words.

Great saints have greatly developed powers of intuition. They can perceive or understand certain things that ordinary people cannot.

Buddhist writer Christmas Humphreys says that intuition is a reliable guide in life. It can be supplemented by reasoning.

When it is developed, intuition tells us what you should do on that day. It also helps us in choosing between alternatives.

Mahatma Gandhi said he sometimes heard an inner voice (or the still small voice or the voice of the conscience) telling him what to do in a given situation. He said you could hear this voice clearly only if you made an effort to purify yourself. (Purity refers to the near absence of thoughts of desire and animosity.)

When Hindu-Muslim riots broke out during Partition, Gandhi heard an inner voice telling him to go on a fast to urge people to stop the violence. He said he would believe his inner voice even if the entire world was sceptical. Some people make false claims about hearing the inner voice, but it does exist and can guide us, he said.

* * * * *

4.

On Writing and Reading

Khushwant Singh on writing—Luann Budd on journal writing—Julia Cameron on journal writing and creativity—Great suggestions from Anne Lamott—Lessons from Premchand's short story 'The Writer'—Excessive reading can make us feel dull—Characteristics of a good inspirational book—On editing a write-up

4. a. Khushwant Singh on writing

In his autobiography, 'Truth, Love and a Little Malice', Khushwant Singh discusses what it takes to become a writer. The foremost requirement is a passion to become one. You need to read contemporary and classic literature widely, he said. You should have the ability to sit for hours if need be staring at a blank paper and you need the determination not to get up till it is filled with writing. (He wrote this before computers become widely used. Nowadays one can rephrase it: You need the determination not to get up till you have written say 300 words on your computer.) He said initially the writing quality will be poor, but gradually it will improve. Writing a daily diary or long emails to friends will give you practice. You should try to write regularly.

He said many sensitive people write poetry in their teens or youth. Later they attempt to write short stories or novels but they give up midway as they do not have the determination or faith in themselves to complete the work.

He said writing is a solitary profession in which no one can help you except yourself. There is no Guru-Chela (mentor-guide) relationship in the writing world, he said. You have to teach yourself to write. Wide reading and regular practice in writing are a great help in learning how to write well.

Khushwant Singh also said that he got a tremendous sense of fulfilment from writing, which he did not get in other professions he tried: law, teaching and diplomacy.

Nowadays many writers have a full-time job and write for one or two hours daily in their free time. They do not try to support themselves on the uncertain income from writing. Nirad Chaudhuri suggested this path to young men or women with intellectual ambitions: Take up a job and write in your spare time. He said it would be better if you can find a job as a teacher, university lecturer, journalist, or advertising copy writer. Such jobs would prevent your intellectual faculties from rusting and also provide a regular income. You can then read and write for two hours in your free time.

4. b. Luann Budd on journal writing

Luann Budd has written an insightful book titled 'Journal Keeping: Writing for Spiritual Growth'. Here are some points from the book which Anil found particularly appealing.

She says that some people prefer to write on a computer while others do so in a lined notebook with a pen. Anil prefers white sheets or a notebook with unruled, white paper. You have to use that method which works best for you.

The first guideline is to keep your journal private. From the beginning should have the intention that what you write will be for your eyes only. Otherwise, you will not be honest in what you write. If there is a piece of journal writing which you would like to share with readers, you can rewrite it in a suitable way for publication. You have to check grammar, spelling and logic in the piece, give a suitable headline and try to write the important or interesting point in the first one or two paragraphs.

If you have a desk where you usually do your writing, you might like to tidy it up at night so that you can begin writing straightaway the next morning, suggests Budd. You can keep your journal notebook, pens (or white paper and pencils) in a bag so that you do not have to search for them each time you sit down to write.

Luann Budd makes an important point: Writing is not merely the recording of thoughts, but the process of writing facilitates and promotes thought. In other words, as you try to write on a subject, you are able to think about it.

The process of writing sustains enquiry. By writing, you are able to get a better understanding of the subject.

Luann Budd says that it is better not to be too structured when you plan to write. When you are writing in a journal, allow yourself the freedom to write in any way you like. After a few weeks or so, you will know what works best for you. Even this method of writing which you have selected will change over a period of months or years. It does not matter how you write, the important thing is to write regularly.

(If you are unable to get hold of the book, visit her website https://journalkeeping.org.)

4. c. Julia Cameron on journal writing and creativity

In her book 'The Artist's Way', Julia Cameron stresses on two things to revive one's creativity: the morning pages and the artist's date.

The morning pages are three pages of longhand writing, strictly stream of consciousness, she said. We should write whatever comes to mind without censoring, worrying about grammar or spelling, without trying to write well. We should not try to produce a work of art, but just put on paper whatever comes to mind. We should do this first thing in the morning after waking up. Done over a period of a few months, writing morning pages revives our creativity and connects us to a source of wisdom within. Writing morning pages may seem to be a pointless exercise, but it works. They have helped many people in recovering their creativity, she said.

The artist's date is an activity done for say two hours once a week. We can spend time on activities such as reading a good book, visiting a museum or a photo exhibition, watching a classic movie or even taking a long walk. The artist's date should preferably be done alone.

The entire book is great, but if we are short of time, we can read just one chapter titled 'The Basic Tools' twice. It must be mentioned that Julia Cameron's methods are intended not just for those who wish to become professional writers, but anyone who wishes to revive their creativity such as teachers, homemakers, screenwriters, cooks or clerks.

Most people who do journal writing begin by doing freewriting, that is, they write whatever comes to mind without censoring or worrying about grammar or spelling. They just want to express their thoughts and feelings. They feel an inner urge to write what's on their mind. The only difference is that they do not necessarily do it in the mornings. Some people like to write at night. After reading Julia Cameron, they will realise that they should just write whatever comes to mind without trying to write well.

After some months of doing freewriting, we may try to do focused freewriting, that is, write a few questions on top of the page and then write one or two pages about any one of the questions (or subject). You can do freewriting, but try to stick to the subject. Like many professional writers, Julia Cameron stresses writing in the mornings when the mind is fresh.

4. d. Great suggestions from Anne Lamott

Anne Lamott gives some excellent suggestions on writing in her book 'Bird by Bird' a few of which are mentioned here.

We have to realise that the first draft is primitive. Almost all writers write bad first drafts, she says. We should not think that a good writer comes up with perfect sentences in the first attempt. The first drafts of even great writers are shitty. We can improve upon the first draft the next day. After that we can read it once, making corrections and send it. This is a point that the great economist John Kenneth Galbraith also made in his essay 'Writing, Typing and Economics'.

The second point she stresses is that we should think in terms of short assignments. Thinking about how we will write the entire book may overwhelm us. We can just have a rough idea how we will carry on. We can break up the entire task into short, manageable assignments so that the complete project does not look impossible.

She also says that while writing we will often not have a clear idea of what the final product will be like. We have a rough idea, we carry on and the final product surprises us. EL Doctorow said that writing a novel is like driving a car at night. You see just a little distance ahead which is lit by the headlights. You don't see long stretches of the road. But you can make the entire journey in this way.

She stresses that we should not try to be perfect. Otherwise, the book or the piece may never get written. You have to keep working but accept a certain degree of imperfection.

Lamott writes about her own experience when she used to write food reviews for a magazine. On the first day she went to the restaurant with her friends. She took notes about the food and what they said.

The next day she selected the points she wanted to make as the lead as well as the conclusion. She then wrote a second draft, revised the entire thing once and sent it. When we have to write for publication, we can remember what she said: The first draft is bad, the second is better and the third draft shines.

4. e. Lessons from Premchand's short story 'The Writer'

The short story 'The Writer' (Lekhak) by the great Hindi writer Premchand has valuable lessons for aspiring writers.

In the short story, Pravin is a writer who has written several articles in newspapers and magazines and is invited by a wealthy man to a party. He is working on his masterpiece which he feels would bring him fame and adequate money. He lives in poverty with his wife.

He wakes up in the morning and as there is no milk or sugar at home, he prepares black tea. He sees that his wife is sleeping and does not want to wake her up. He begins to write.

He usually works almost the entire day on his masterpiece. Today he tells his wife that he is happy as a wealthy man has invited him to a party where he can meet many eminent citizens. The party is in honour of a judge who has been appointed recently. Pravin composes a poem to welcome him. His wife dissuades him from going to the party as he does not have decent clothes. He tells his wife that the wealthy see the personal qualities of a person and not his clothes. His wife is not convinced but he decides to go. He tells her that every writer has a hunger to get recognition and appreciation.

In the evening he goes to the party in his ill-fitting clothes. The guard asks him whether he has an invitation. Pravin gets offended as the guard has asked only him and not the others. His wife seemed to be right about clothes.

At the party the wealthy man introduces him to several eminent citizens as a noted poet. Pravin is introduced to a gentleman who has written articles in English newspapers. He asks Pravin whether he has read Byron and Shelley and tells him that if he translates these poets into Hindi he would do a great honour to the language. Pravin considers himself to be a good poet in his own right and does not think it is an honour to translate English poems into Hindi. The admirer of the English poets is offended and the host tries to tell Pravin that the other person is a highly respected man. Pravin is offended.

The wealthy host introduces him to some other persons who have no interest in poets. Doctors have no interest in treating him free and lawyers feel Pravin cannot get them customers. When Pravin is introduced, they say, “Oh, you are a poet” and move away. They feel that they have no use for a person who lives his life in the imagination.

Pravin feels insulted by this time. When the chief guest arrives, the host comes to him and asks him whether he has written a poem in his honour. Pravin says he is not a paid performer. The host tells him that he could perhaps read out an ancient poet which he remembers. Pravin is feeling bad because of the way he has been treated this evening and decides to leave.

At home, his wife asks him whether he was treated well and enjoyed the party. Pravin says he has learnt his lesson: My hut is my palace and a writer's real work is to write.

What lessons could we draw? An aspiring writer should be prepared for financial difficulties in the beginning of his or her career. For this reason, most experienced writers advise aspirants to take up a job which leaves about two hours of free time for them to write.

The second lesson is that a writer should give up the desire for social status because of his writing. She should not worry too much about being respected by wealthy and influential people and instead should focus on writing well.

4. f. Excessive reading can make us feel dull

Albert Einstein said, "Reading, after a certain age, diverts the mind too much from its creative pursuits. Any man who reads too much and uses his own brain too little falls into lazy habits of thinking."

People over the age of 40 who spend a lot of time on reading can try to cut down on it and see the effects. But, of course, this suggestion is only for people who read a lot.

Younger people should read widely for say 10 or 20 years. Reading is one of the best ways to educate ourselves.

But there are some people who tend to read too much. They can observe a reading fast during the first few hours after waking up. It is particularly important to avoid reading news immediately after waking up. On a day when we face some kind of mental strain, we can avoid reading till say lunch time.

We tend to read a lot out of habit and feel that if we do not do so, we will become intellectually stagnant. We have the belief that we would become an accomplished intellectual only if we read a lot.

But instead of reading widely, we can cut down on it to some extent and focus on journal writing. Writing engages the mind as much as reading. Writing is a method of thinking.

Mahatma Gandhi said that it is wrong to store unnecessary information in one's brain. He said, "We should remember that non-possession is a principle applicable to thoughts as wells as to things. A man who fills his mind with useless knowledge violates that inestimable principle. Thoughts, which turn us away from God and do not turn us towards Him, constitute impediments in our way."

The German philosopher Arthur Schopenhauer said that if one reads almost the whole day without thinking much, one gradually loses one's capacity to think independently.

Russian writer Leo Tolstoy has said that if you can think independently, you need not read much. He said he knew several scholars who had not read much.

What is important for writing is to have a certain spiritual discipline in one's life. A spiritual writer can avoid alcohol, tobacco and sensuality and can meditate, go for walks and interact positively with others.

Many people are not able to read much because office work drains their mental energy. They may be doing some kind of mental work such as editing which requires concentration and thought. On a day when they are not mentally exhausted, they can skim through parts of their favourite books. It is better to do this later in the day and not in the mornings. They can also skim through news on say the BBC App or other news site for say 10 minutes. This will not tire them.

Despite a heavy schedule of office work, you can write the next morning. Writing does not exhaust the mind but rejuvenates it. Writing would be as pleasant an activity as reading and could be even more satisfying.

4. g. Characteristics of a good inspirational book

What are the characteristics of a good inspirational book? The book needs to be interesting and useful to the reader. The reader should be able to apply some of the ideas to her own life. It should give her a better understanding of reality and fill her with the determination to keep on trying.

The book should make her realise the benefits of self-control and leading a simple life.

You should be able to able to understand the sentences and paragraphs easily without the need to look up the dictionary online or offline frequently. It would be useful if the sentences are short and in subject-verb-object pattern for they are easy to understand. Most of the words need to be short and simple. The sentences in a paragraph ought to be connected with each other.

Reading becomes more interesting if the reader is able to visualize what he is reading. The use of concrete nouns instead of abstract ones helps in this objective.

Readers like books that have human or animal characters with which they can identify. The writer can present her ideas through these characters.

For a spiritual book, it is important that the writer presents honestly what he or she truly thinks. The writer ought not falsify her feelings. We can perhaps call this emotional sincerity.

A spiritual writer needs to have a sense of morality. He should not promote violence, sensuality or a luxurious lifestyle.

The writer can write the book on the basis of her reading, thinking, and experience. But she should present only those truths that she has found true from her experience or faith.

But while writing an inspirational article or book, you should think of what satisfies you. Write what pleases you, what satisfies you. Just see that your sentences are intelligible to be reader. But don't think of the reader too much. If you write in a manner that satisfies you, then many readers too are going to like it.

4. h. On editing a write-up

A simple method of editing short pieces is to read it once, write an introductory paragraph and then correct the sentences, one at a time.

How do we write the intro? While reading the story once, we make the five Ws and an H bold (Answers to what, where, who, when, why and how.) We can then write one or two sentences containing these facts.

If the writeup is not a news report but a feature, then we try to put the most interesting point in the introductory paragraphs. So, in a news report we put the most important point in the first para and in a feature story, we keep the most interesting point in the beginning.

Then we can correct the rest of the sentences, bearing in mind George Orwell's rules: avoid cliches, jargon, cut out superfluous words, prefer active voice and short words. We should see that the sentences in a paragraph are linked. And it is better to use concrete expressions (things we can visualise) rather than abstract ones in our sentences. We must never use words whose meaning we are not sure of.

After editing the entire story, we can read it once to remove any typos or things we might have overlooked. We can also give a headline.

When the story is relatively clean, we can read it once making changes wherever required. We can make those parts of sentences or sentences bold that need to be changed after some thought. While going through the story a second time, we can pause at the portions made bold, think and carry out the changes.

When we have to edit our own writing, it is better to give a day's gap after writing. Then we will be able to look at the piece with fresh eyes and edit it.

It is useful to know how to type with all fingers. It saves time and is more efficient. We also need to know the commands of the word processing software such as MS Word or Open Office.

We must refer to online dictionaries when required. We can read 'The Elements of Style' by Strunk and White and also George Orwell's essay 'Politics and the English language' from time to time. Apart from the valuable suggestions that they contain, they will increase our enthusiasm for writing and editing.

* * * * *

5.

The Simple Spiritual Practices of Japa, Pranayama

Japa, a suitable practice for householders—Evolution of Anil's japa practice—Mahatma Gandhi on Ramanama—Pranayama and meditation apps

5. a. Japa, a suitable practice for householders

The repetition of mantras or japa seems to be the best spiritual practice for people who are married and have a job or business. They can do japa for 20-40 minutes in the morning and then whenever they get free time. Japa is the easiest way to attain God-realisation, said Swami Sivananda.

Hindus can use a maala or rosary of 108 beads. In other religions, the rosary has a different number of beads. Sikhs also use a smaller maala with fewer beads for japa or namasmaran.

Hindus can use the middle finger and thumb of the right hand for rolling the beads. Initially, we need a rosary, but after a few months of practice, we can do manasika japa or mental japa. In his book Japa Yoga, Swami Sivananda said that we should preferably face the north or the east while doing japa and the maala should not hang below the navel.

It is easier to concentrate on japa when you sit alone in a quiet room. If you find it hard to concentrate while doing mental repetition, you should use a rosary.

All that is needed for doing japa is the faith that it is beneficial and the determination to do it. Too much reasoning, thinking or discussion on whether japa is beneficial is counterproductive. You can do it for say 10 minutes daily for a fortnight and see the benefits.

We can use a mantra given by our spiritual teacher or if that is not possible, we can select a suitable mantra of the deity whom we have faith in. Hare Krishnas chant the mantra: Hare Krishna, Hare Krishna, Krishna, Krishna, Hare Hare/ Hare Rama, Hare Rama, Rama Rama, Hare Hare. Those who have faith in Lord Shiva chant the mantra Om Namah Shivay. The mantra for Lord Ganesha, the God of wisdom and worldly success, is Om Gam Ganpatye Namah. The mantra of the goddess of learning is Om Sri Sarasvatyai Namah. The mantra for the goddess of wealth is Om Sri Mahalakshmyai Namah.

Mahatma Gandhi used to repeat the name of Lord Rama. He did not follow any spiritual practices like pranayama or yoga asanas, but he repeated the name of Ram. Mahatma Gandhi said Christians can repeat "Jesus" and Muslims can repeat "Allah." Islam has a rich tradition of Zikr in which the person repeats either "Allah" or short phrases from the Quran. Muslims can consult an Imam for guidance.

It is better to stick to one mantra. Changing mantras frequently is not advisable.

During the morning japa one should sit down or walk but not lie down. Later in the day, if you are tired, you can lie down and do japa. But while lying down, you should not use a rosary and should repeat the mantra mentally.

Idle talk, lustful thoughts or a heavy meal can make it difficult to do japa. We can wait for a while after a meal before doing japa. And it is best to avoid unnecessary talking while doing japa otherwise it would be hard to focus.

It is better to avoid tea or coffee during the first 20 or 30 minutes of japa in the morning. Later in the day you can perhaps have tea before a japa session. But it must be pointed out that Hare Krishnas say that you must avoid tea and coffee. Of course, they also advise us to avoid tobacco and alcohol, which are stronger than tea or coffee.

Commuting time in a Metro train or bus is excellent for doing manasic japa. But you may not be able to do japa if someone is playing music or watching a video or talking loudly in the Metro train.

Japa is therapeutic. When you are thinking hard or worried and distracted, doing japa for a while will focus the mind and prevent unnecessary thinking. You will get peace and inner strength. Japa and reading chapter 2 of the Gita were the sources of inner strength of Mahatma Gandhi.

At bedtime you can do 10 minutes of japa sitting on the bed. It is an excellent way to relax and fall asleep if you suffer from insomnia.

The Gita says that God is easily attainable by one who constantly remembers Him. Japa or mantra meditation is one of the best ways of remembering God.

5. b. Evolution of Anil's japa practice

In the year 2006 when Anil was facing a worldly problem related to his job, a Pandit advised him to do japa daily for two weeks. As he did not have a rosary, he began to do japa using gram seeds. The repetition of any mantra or name of God is called japa.

He found that japa focused his mind, reduced worries and gave him inner strength. So, he decided to make it a part of his daily life.

In 2007 he bought a maala (rosary) and began to do japa for some time daily. After using a maala for six months, he was able to do manasika japa (mental repetition) without a maala.

Earlier, he used to whisper the mantra or repeat it aloud. Later he began to do it silently.

After some more months of practice, he was able to concentrate on japa in the Metro train or bus when there was no music playing nearby. He was able to do 15 minutes of japa while commuting to office.

Anil found that the best time to do japa is in the mornings just after waking up and brushing his teeth. He usually did 20 to 30 minutes of japa before beginning his daily activities.

He sometimes faced obstacles in doing japa. When he was worried or under stress, he found it difficult to concentrate. When lustful thoughts were an obstacle, he made an effort to get away from the spot and repeat mantras for a while. With some effort he was able to overcome negative or lustful thoughts.

He sometimes also did mantra writing or likhit japa. He wrote a particular mantra with a pen till he filled up one or two pages in an exercise book. He did not speak while writing the mantras though, if necessary, he sometimes got up from his seat. It was an excellent practice that helped him to focus and gave him inner strength.

After many years of practice, he now does japa for some time in the morning and then whenever he gets leisure. A Hindu pandit advised him that when he uses a maala, he should either sit or stand up. But when he is tired and is lying down, then he can repeat the mantra mentally without using a rosary.

Japa has been a source of inner strength to him during his daily struggles. When he looks back over the years, he realizes that acquiring the habit of doing japa daily was one the greatest spiritual achievements of his life.

5. c. Mahatma Gandhi on Ramanama

Mahatma Gandhi was afraid of ghosts in his childhood. A nurse told him that there were no ghosts but if he was afraid, he could repeat the name of Lord Rama.

As he grew in age and wisdom, the practice became habitual. It requires effort to get into the habit of repeating Ramanama, but when once that is done, it is the greatest thing one can possess, he said.

One can repeat Ramanama silently while in conversation, while doing brain work or when one is suddenly worried. And one can do it mentally when one does not have a rosary. He said that when Ramanama was enshrined in the heart, it means the rebirth of man.

He said that conservation of the vital force (celibacy or brahmacharya) can transform the body. When celibacy is combined with Ramanama, the results are miraculous, said Gandhi. Ramanama can also cure psychosomatic ailments.

5. d. Pranayama and meditation apps

Pranayama is a breathing exercise that helps you to focus and relax the mind. It soothes the mind when one is worried or is thinking too much. Yogis say that it is excellent for health.

The method is as follows: Sit down. Close the right nostril with the right thumb and inhale slowly from the left nostril. Then close the left nostril also with the little and ring fingers and retain the breath for a short while. Exhale slowly from the right nostril. Inhale from the right nostril, close it with the thumb, hold the breath. Exhale from the left nostril. This is one pranayama.

Begin with five pranayamas. In the beginning do not retain the breath after inhaling. Later you can increase the number of pranayamas to 20. Some people face problems while doing pranayama. They should not retain the breath. They can consult a yoga teacher if necessary.

Pranayama has certain similarities with breathing meditation. You can enjoy some of the benefits of breathing meditation by doing it. It should preferably be done when the stomach is relatively empty.

Swami Ramdev and Sri Sri Ravi Shankar are among the many yogis who have popularized the practice in India.

Nowadays, many people meditate using an app on their phone. Several men and women in the West who were interested in meditation came to India or the Buddhist countries, learnt meditation and observed spiritual disciplines. They created apps which combined ancient and modern techniques of meditation. Some of the popular meditation apps are Headspace, Calm and Wake Up. You can use them for relaxing, developing concentration, or falling asleep.

* * * * *

6.

On Staying Physically Healthy

Suggestions for good health from Mahatma Gandhi—The gift of good health—On avoiding gluttony—Psychological benefits of walking—How Anil gave up tobacco addiction

6. a. Suggestions for good health from Mahatma Gandhi

Though written many years ago, it can still be beneficial to read the booklet 'Key to Health' by Mahatma Gandhi. It discusses food, intoxicants and brahmacharya or celibacy but does not have chapters on physical exercise, insomnia and fasting which people might like to read today.

Gandhi preferred wheat to other cereals. Excessive sugar consumption must be avoided, he said.

He was in favour of a vegetarian diet, but felt that milk was necessary for vegetarians to provide animal proteins and several vitamins needed for tissue repair.

Fruits of the season should be a part of our daily diet. We can also have the juice of one or two lemons with a glass of water daily.

Pulses or dal are a rich source of protein, but are slightly hard to digest. It is better to have dal for lunch and not dinner.

Some fats and oils are also needed. We can have a small quantity of butter or ghee in our diet.

Seasonal vegetables are a rich source of vitamins and minerals. Some vegetables can be eaten raw.

One can have three meals a day, but several doctors nowadays are in favour of having small meals more frequently.

According to the booklet, there is a school of thought that says that limited consumption of alcohol is good for health. Gandhi did not agree with this and said that there is a danger that one would increase alcohol intake when one is under stress or tension or is depressed.

Tobacco is the worst among intoxicants, said Leo Tolstoy. It's one of the most habit-forming substances and once it is formed, most people are never able to give it up. As it is convenient to carry and use, many youngsters use tobacco to reduce stress. But tobacco use is a major cause of cancer.

Two or three cups of tea might help hard workers but excessive consumption is harmful as it contains caffeine and tannin (which is the same substance that is used in processing leather).

Gandhi felt that we should try to control desire to stay mentally and physically healthy. We should stay busy most of the time as when we are idle, lustful thoughts may arise.

We can repeat a mantra or the name of God in order to prevent negative thoughts from arising and also to get divine grace. Eating just for taste, overeating and consumption of meat and fish may make self-control harder.

Gandhi said that in his opinion, a brisk walk in the open is the best form of exercise. But one can also learn a few yoga asanas and practice them for say 15 minutes every morning. Nowadays, health-conscious people like to do five workouts at the gym every week.

Insomnia was not widely prevalent a century ago, so he does not include a chapter on sleep in the booklet. But if one stays active during the daytime, avoids excessive consumption of tea and coffee in the evenings or nights, avoids hard brain work at bedtime and relaxes by doing meditation or light reading, then insomnia is not likely to trouble us.

6. b. The gift of good health

What is good health? In a lay person's terms, we can say that we are healthy when we get adequate sleep, have regular bowel movements, an absence of physical discomfort or pain, and are able to do our routine work satisfactorily.

We can stay healthy by paying attention to diet and exercise. The state of mind or the nature of our thoughts also affects our physical health.

A balanced diet that includes carbohydrates, proteins, fats, vitamins, minerals, water and roughage or fibre should be taken. Spiritual aspirants can preferably take a vegetarian diet that includes a glass of milk or a bowl of curd, and plenty of fruits. Opinion is divided on whether spiritual aspirants should have eggs. Mahatma Gandhi did not himself have eggs but said that they could be considered vegetarian. Eggs are a rich source of animal protein and vitamins. However, ISKCON and several other Hindu organisations advise us to avoid meat, fish and eggs. Spiritual teachers suggest that we avoid excessive sexual intercourse in order to stay healthy, but several doctors do not agree with this view.

If we are addicted to tobacco or alcohol, we can make a determined effort to give them up. Tea and coffee help hard workers, but are harmful in excess.

Quite a few people with sedentary habits have constipation nowadays. They can cure it by including plenty of fibre in their diet and going for walks. Fruits such as papaya, apples, vegetables such as carrots and cabbage, and whole wheat bread or chapatti are rich in fiber. We can have Triphala or Isabgol at night to prevent constipation. It is better to have a light meal at night. Bhujang asana, Salabh asana and Dhanur asana help remove constipation (You can look up a yoga book). We should try to avoid excessive intake of sugar, fried food and items made from refined flour.

Doctors advise us to have eight glasses of water daily. This would help remove toxins from the body. But even water should not be had in excess, say Ayurveda practitioners.

Twenty to 30 minutes of physical exercise should be a part of our daily routine. Walking is a pleasant exercise that not only keeps us physically fit, but also soothes our mind.

We can go for a walk or do exercises on at least five days a week.

When we fall ill, we should be honest with our doctor and tell him or her our symptoms and then follow the advice. It might be useful to write down our symptoms before going to the doctor.

If we try to stay healthy, we will be able to make the most of our lives. Good health is required not only to do our work properly, but also for our spiritual and mental pursuits.

6. c. On avoiding gluttony

Siddhartha tries to avoid overeating and eating just for taste. He ensures that he has a glass of milk and plenty of fruits daily.

When he wants to have a snack, he tries to have it with his meals. Otherwise, it becomes difficult to exercise self-control and he tends to eat a variety of snacks.

He tries to have just a plate of fruits for dinner. But sometimes when he is mentally exhausted or under stress, he has a proper meal so that he gets sound sleep and is able to overcome fatigue.

While having meals, he tries to stay silent or avoid unnecessary talking. This enables him to eat slowly and mindfully.

He sometimes breaks these rules and tries not to feel guilty about it. But he realizes that control over what he eats and adequate exercise will keep him healthy.

One of the precepts for Buddhist monks is not to eat after midday. The Dalai Lama has lunch and evening tea, but no dinner. But sometimes he has a few biscuits at night. It is generally a good idea to have a light meal at night.

When Siddhartha is under stress, he eats snacks or sweets just for taste. The problem is that when he eats a little just for taste, self-control diminishes and he tends to have a variety of snacks and sweets, but as long as this is occasional, it is fine.

A few years ago, he became vegetarian, largely for spiritual reasons. There is good reason for considering eggs as vegetarian as they are a good source of protein and other nutrients. But Siddhartha has decided to have just a glass of milk daily and no eggs. He also tries to include plenty of fibre in his diet to prevent constipation.

It is said that including meat and fish in one's diet arouses passion and makes one aggressive. If one wants to control passion and anger, it might be a good idea to cut down on non-vegetarian food. But too much should not be made of this. The primary purpose of food is to keep us healthy and we should eat such foods that keep us healthy.

6. d. Psychological benefits of walking

After his morning meditation, Anil feels the need to go for a short walk. There might be negative thoughts and a feeling of lethargy which walking removes.

He sometimes goes up and down the stairs a few times, but that is not as pleasant as a walk in the open.

A walk adds to one's sense of wellbeing and also facilitates bowel movements. Anil prefers to meditate before going for a walk. Going out of the house makes him focus outward and not inward. During the walk he starts thinking of worldly matters. For these reasons, he prefers to meditate for 20 minutes before going for a walk.

When Anil is worried, a walk helps him to think over issues bothering him. But to think, one must not walk too briskly. As Anil walks, his thoughts are gradually sorted out and he may intuitively get a solution to his problems. The only time he does not go for a walk is when the weather is hot.

Playwright Charan Das Sidhu said he often got ideas for his plays during long walks. He was a college lecturer and during his vacations he sometimes went long distances on foot. He once walked from village to village in the guise of a bangle seller and said it was great fun. On another occasion, when he was on a long walk, a group of students commented that he seemed to be Hiuen Tsang (the 7th Century Buddhist traveller) and he liked this comment.

Mahatma Gandhi said that he stayed healthy in England because of his habit of going for walks. A brisk walk in the open was the best form of exercise, he said.

There is an Ayurveda practitioner who treats mental illness by giving medicines to aid sleep and digestion. He takes his young patients for walks and talks to them.

The spiritual guru Bhagwan Rajneesh had developed several methods of meditation, one of which was walking meditation. Hindu pundits say that one can repeat mantras while walking which is a pleasant experience if the streets are clean.

In the city of Mathura in India, spiritually inclined people come and go around the entire city on foot chanting mantras. Going around the city walking is called a parikrama in Hindi. You start at a temple and then come back to the same spot which is a pleasant spiritual experience.

Many writers are fond of walking. Ruskin Bond said, "I was really a walking person—and was to remain so all my life."

The words of philosopher Soren Kierkegaard are inspiring: "Above all, do not lose your desire to walk. Everyday, I walk myself into a state of well-being and walk away from every illness. I have walked myself into my best thoughts, and I know of no thought so burdensome that one cannot walk away from it. But by sitting still, and the more one sits still, the closer one comes to feeling ill. Thus, if one just keeps on walking, everything will be all right."

6. e. How Anil gave up tobacco addiction

Anil began to smoke and chew tobacco when he failed in the final year university exams and felt that the future was bleak. Within a few months he was addicted to tobacco.

He smoked or chewed tobacco to stimulate his mind, feel that he was in control of the situation, get a feeling of being aware, and also to facilitate bowel movements. He found that tobacco helped him to concentrate and remove mental fatigue. It enabled him to focus while having a conversation or doing a solitary activity like journal writing.

After a year or so, he did not get any benefit when he smoked but got withdrawal symptoms when he did not. He was aware that smoking causes cancer. He had a child who was a few years old and he did not want to get cancer and make him suffer.

Anil began to read literature on how to give up tobacco: The book 'Overcoming Addiction' by Dr Deepak Chopra, an article by Swami Sivananda and the essay 'Why Do Men Stupefy Themselves' by Leo Tolstoy.

Dr Chopra said that a person who consumes tobacco, alcohol or drugs is in reality seeking a spiritual experience though he is seeking it in the wrong place as opposed to where he can actually find it such as meditation. Dr Chopra says that the first step in trying to give up tobacco addiction is to smoke with full awareness. You should quietly focus on the effect the cigarette is having on you and not smoke while, for instance, watching television or chatting with someone.

Swami Sivananda says that you should give up smoking or chewing tobacco all of a sudden and not gradually. Attempts to give it up gradually are generally unsuccessful. People who have smoked for say 15 or 20 years have been able to kick the habit. Anil had had the habit for 18 years so he drew inspiration from these words of Swami Sivananda.

Anil also visited a psychiatrist who gave some pills to combat withdrawal symptoms. But he was not fully successful.

Leo Tolstoy, who was a heavy smoker and drinker in his youth, said that if you give it up suddenly, the suffering lasts for only about a week. After that one's mind gradually begins to function normally even without tobacco.

Once when he had taken one week's leave from office, Anil sat on the bed and made a resolution to give up the habit even if he became mentally troubled. For seven days he sat on the bed, leaving it only to go to the washroom or to the park for a walk or to have his meals. He did pranayama (breathing exercises) for a while. He found that he was not in the right mental state to read. He wrote a few short sentences in his diary which he kept beside himself. It was terrible for one week when he feared the worst. He thought that the symptoms would never go away. But after four days they began to subside. His wife was a source of moral support.

After a week, the craving was gone and he could work in office without chewing or smoking tobacco though he faced some difficulties. More than 15 years have passed since that week and a mild wish to smoke or chew remains, but Anil resists the temptation, realising that giving up tobacco was an achievement in his life.

This was his method of giving up tobacco, and yours could be different. What is important is to get professional advice if necessary and have determination and faith in yourself.

* * * * *

7.

Staying at the Peak of Our Mental Powers

On staying mentally fit—Some basic books on psychology—Philippa Perry on mental health—Thomas Szasz on mental illness—Dr Sudhir Kakar on psychotherapy—The contribution of Sigmund Freud—On client-centred therapy—Viktor Frankl on having a meaningful life—Understanding schizophrenia—Dale Carnegie's self-help book

7. a. On staying mentally fit

Adequate sleep and freedom from worry or sadness will help to keep us mentally healthy. Getting sound sleep is important for mental health. For this, we should avoid tea, coffee and hard mental work at bedtime. It is better to have a light dinner. If we cannot fall asleep at night, we can sit in a chair and meditate, pray or do light reading till we feel sleepy. If worries prevent us from falling asleep, we can write down our problems and what we plan to do about them the next day in a few sentences. Or we can pray. If a person over 40 years gets about six hours of sleep, he or she can function normally.

We can do 20 to 40 minutes of mantra meditation daily. This will give us inner strength to face obstacles, peace of mind and allow us to receive God's grace.

We should try not to oppose evil. We can stay silent when people criticise us, but if necessary, we can give an explanation. We can also have brahmacharya or celibacy as our ideal.

Writing down our thoughts and feelings is therapeutic. You can write whatever comes to mind without censoring and worrying about grammar or spelling.

When you face a serious problem, you can talk to an expert, a psychologist, or psychiatrist. And when you are worried, you can pray. God listens to all sincere prayers.

Finally, you should do total surrender to the Lord. As Swami Sivananda suggests, you can say mentally, "I am an instrument in the hands of God. God does everything for my own good. Let Thy will be done."

It is important to live in the present. As William Osler suggests, we should try to "live in day-tight compartments." This means that we focus on doing today's tasks and not worry about the future or have regrets about the past. As the Bible says, "Have no anxiety about tomorrow. Tomorrow will take care of itself."

7. b. Some basic books on psychology

Anil read a few books to get a basic idea about psychology and noted down his observations. This was his method and yours would be different.

He first read Dr Janette Rainwater's 'You're In Charge: A Guide to Becoming Your Own Therapist'. The book discusses the art of self-observation, fantasy, relationships, journal writing, autobiography writing, dream analysis, meditation, the art of being in the now, physical health and death. It is a self-help book and may perhaps be more useful for overcoming psychological problems than textbooks on psychology. After reading this book, one can move on to introductory books on psychology.

He then read 'Introduction to Psychology' by Clifford Morgan, Richard A King, John R Weiss and John Schopler. He also read parts of 'Psychology' by Robert A Baron and Girishwar Misra. One can read the chapters on abnormal psychology, therapy and in particular the sections on Sigmund Freud, Carl Rogers, Abraham Maslow, and Viktor Frankl. One can read how one can make an assessment of psychological disorders and their classification such as anxiety, depression and schizophrenia. Then one can read about the modern systems of classification of mental disorders. The chapters on personality, motivation and thinking are interesting. One can also read about the problems of old age.

One book all adults can read is 'Man's Search for Meaning' by Viktor Frankl.

Dr Sanjeev Prasad's 'Journey of the Soul' helps us understand some spiritual issues including death and gives a glimpse of a psychiatrist's life.

Those who wish to understand a therapist's life can try 'Book of Memory' by psychoanalyst and writer Dr Sudhir

Kakar. The book is interesting and insightful, but the style of writing is a bit scholarly.

7. c. Philippa Perry on mental health

Her book titled 'How to Stay Sane' has four chapters. They are on self-observation, relationships, stress and what's the story. The most important chapter is on self-observation which suggests that we should keep a daily journal, a dream journal, meditate and pray for developing self-awareness.

Dr Janette Rainwater says that we should ask ourselves the following questions from time to time to develop self-awareness: What am I thinking? How am I feeling? What am I doing? How am I breathing? What do I want for myself? Perry also stresses on asking these questions.

In the chapter on positive stress, Perry suggests that we should try to read, learn new things, and do physical exercises. We can cut down on watching television, movies and news as they often have a negative content.

The last chapter suggests that therapy is successful when a person changes her perception of who she is and what she plans to do in life.

Philippa Perry's book is a part of the School of Life series edited by the philosopher Alain de Botton.

7. d. Thomas Szasz on mental illness

Thomas Szasz, an original thinker in the field of psychiatry, says it is wrong to call psychological disorders as a "mental illness" as they cannot be diagnosed by examining cells, tissues and organs. Psychological disorders refer to disapproved thoughts, feelings and behaviours, he felt.

He is opposed to involuntary hospitalisation of a person on the basis of the opinion of a psychiatrist or mental health professional. But no person can be excused of lawbreaking or other offences just because a psychiatrist diagnoses him to be insane.

The relationship between a psychiatrist and a patient should be contractual, he said. At present psychiatry sometimes becomes a method of social control. It must be emphasised, however, that Szasz does not discourage people from visiting psychiatrists.

7. e. Dr Sudhir Kakar on psychotherapy

In his autobiography, India's leading psychoanalyst Dr Sudhir Kakar says that introspection is the royal road to the healing of psychological disorders.

Psychoanalysis originated in the West and was based on the lives of people there. When Dr Kakar began to practise in India, he had to adapt the Western methods to suit Indian conditions.

One needs to be aware of one's inner states in order to be mentally healthy, he says. In the West, the psychiatrist is an expert, a mirror who reflects the client's thoughts and feelings. But in India, patients see a psychologist as a compassionate guru or teacher.

7. f. The contribution of Sigmund Freud

Sigmund Freud was one of the greatest psychologists whose theories are relevant today, more than a century after they were propounded.

He divided the human mind into three parts: the id, the ego and the superego. The id consists of primitive, innate desires which are hidden from consciousness. It corresponds to the "desires" mentioned in religious writings.

The ego is the reasoning part of the brain. The superego refers to our views on what is right or wrong or our sense of morality.

The id consists of needs and urges which seek instant gratification. But there would be a crisis if we try to fulfil some of these desires. The superego tells us which of these and to what extent they should be fulfilled. The ego mediates between id and superego and the individual takes action.

Baron and Misra in their book 'Psychology' give the example of a middle-aged woman who is attracted to her daughter's boyfriend. If these thoughts come to the surface of her mind, she would feel uncomfortable. She might experience anxiety, worry or tension. So, the mind resorts to a defence mechanism. She either forgets these feelings, or rationalizes them, or displaces them or projects them onto others.

7. g. On client-centred therapy

Carl Rogers developed client-centred therapy in the 1970s. An assumption of the system is that each individual is striving for self-actualisation but faces obstacles in the path.

The person undergoing therapy is called a client and not a patient. The therapist talks to him in an atmosphere of acceptance. The client eventually understands his feelings better and is able to cope with situations.

The therapist encourages the client to talk and reflects their thoughts and feelings back to them. The therapist tries to be non-judgmental. The client begins to understand why they feel the way they do. Perhaps somebody had said something earlier in life that prevented them from realizing their potential. They now begin to understand this.

7. h. Viktor Frankl on having a meaningful life

Frankl was a psychotherapist who was imprisoned in concentration camps by the Nazis, and his family members were killed. Upon his release he developed a system of psychotherapy which he explained in a set of books. The books could be summarized in three words: Get to work.

After his release from concentration camps, Frankl developed a system of therapy which he called Logotherapy. The term has its origin in the word logos or meaning. Psychoanalysts try to analyse a person's childhood, but in contrast Frankl focuses on the tasks which they want to achieve in future.

Logotherapy tries to make the patient aware of the tasks before him. Every person needs to have a goal worth striving for.

Frankl said that we need to have the feeling that our life is meaningful in order to stay mentally healthy.

Some existentialist philosophers teach us to endure the meaninglessness of life, but Frankl says we must realize that we cannot understand the meaning of life just by thinking and reasoning.

Some psychiatrists consider a patient's brain to be like a machine which needs to be repaired. But Frankl tries to see the human being behind the machine. Logotherapy does not try to drown a patient's existential frustration by using tranquilising drugs.

Frankl says that no matter what happens to us, we always have some freedom to choose between options. Even when we suffer, we can choose what attitude to adopt towards it.

He says that we can find the meaning of life in three ways: by doing a deed; by loving a person or by experiencing a value such as a work of art; and by accepting suffering with a positive attitude. The first two, work and love, are mentioned in most systems of psychotherapy, but the third, suffering, is rarely discussed by them.

When we face suffering that we cannot avoid, such as an inoperable cancer, then what matters is our attitude towards it. If we see the suffering as a sacrifice for someone we love or as a means of getting closer to God, then it can enrich us.

Frankl says we must not endure suffering if it can be avoided. For example, there is no point in enduring a cancer that can be cured by surgery.

He gives an example. An elderly general practitioner was depressed when his wife whom he deeply loved died. The therapist told him that if he had died first, his wife would have had to suffer. So, in a way he saved her from suffering. Once he saw the situation in this way, he did not suffer much.

Traditional psychotherapy attempts to restore a patient's capacity to work and enjoy life. Logotherapy goes further and teaches the patient to endure suffering with a positive attitude.

Neurosis develops in a person when they feel that their existence is meaningless. A therapist's role is to assist the patient in finding meaning in their life.

Sex is justified, even sanctified, as long as it is a vehicle of love. Love is as primary as phenomenon as sex and is not an epiphenomenon (a secondary phenomenon that occurs alongside a primary phenomenon). You can understand the inner self of a person well only if you love her or him.

7. i. Understanding schizophrenia

Schizophrenia is perhaps the most serious mental illness in which a patient tends to lose touch with other people and reality.

The patients may have difficulty in communicating with others. They may use private words and symbols which are not understood by others.

The person may have delusions (false, illogical beliefs) of persecution or grandeur. The patient may feel that others are conspiring against or persecuting him. He may wrongly believe that "outer forces" are controlling him. He may wrongly believe that he is Jesus Christ or a minister in the government.

Several patients have hallucinations or may hear voices. These symptoms often enable a psychiatrist to diagnose schizophrenia.

Patients do not display emotions of happiness or sorrow. They may have a flat expression all the time.

The patients may also lack motivation. They can sit for hours doing nothing.

The ability to communicate is impaired. If a doctor asks, "How old are you?" the patient may say something that has private significance such as "I am hundreds of years old." If the doctor asks, "Where do you live?" the patient may say "In the netherworld."

The causes of schizophrenia are not fully known. It is believed that there is a genetic predisposition and the illness may be triggered off by severe life stress or problems. The standard treatment is psychotherapy and anti-psychotic drugs.

The objective of this brief section is to give readers an idea about the illness so that if they or somebody they know develops such symptoms, they can contact a psychiatrist or psychologist for help.

7. j. Dale Carnegie's self-help book

Carnegie's 'How to Stop Worrying and Start Living' had a great influence on Anil when he was young. He read it several times and tried to follow its suggestions, noting down some of the things he learnt.

The first lesson is that when we face major problems, we should try to live one day a time and not try to solve our entire life's problems at one go. William Osler said, "Live in day-tight compartments." This means that we should focus on doing what needs to be done today and not worry about the future or have regrets about the past. If we do today's tasks well, the future will automatically be bright.

We can improve our lives by trying to have positive thoughts and eliminate negative thoughts. Roman emperor and philosopher Marcus Aurelius said, "Our life is what our thoughts make it."

If we try to have a positive attitude when we face adversity, we can gain in several ways: We will grow stronger mentally and spiritually. We can convert a minus into a plus. But this does not mean that we invite adversity, merely that we make the right effort when we encounter it.

When a tragedy befalls us, we need to try and come to terms with it: We cannot keep on denying it. We have to accept the situation as it is. Later, we can try to improve upon it.

Carnegie says that there is no need to compare ourselves with others. Every individual is unique in this world. So, we should find ourselves and be ourselves. We can make an assessment of our strengths and weaknesses and accept them. After that we can try to improve on them.

To the extent it is possible, when we are young, we should try to take up an occupation that we like and perhaps not take up something just because of the money and status. Then work will not seem to be burden and we will get satisfaction from it. Thomas Carlyle said, "Blessed is he who has found his work. Let him ask no other blessedness."

Staying busy is a good cure for worry. We can stay busy in work or our hobbies. This is especially important during the first few hours of the day.

"The sovereign cure for worry is religious faith," said the psychologist William James. When we are anxious, we ought to focus on following the teachings of our religion rather than worrying about the many uncertain things in life.

* * * * *

8.

Understanding How Journalists Work

The news story and gathering news-- The experience of reporting—What Rohit learnt at a students' newspaper—On reading the news

8. a. The news story and gathering news

To understand how journalists work, we need to understand what is news, how journalists gather news and how we write a news story.

Newswriting: The first paragraph of a news story, which contains a summary, is called the intro or lead. There are two methods of writing the intro: 1. You note down the answers to the What, Who, Where, When, Why and How (called the 5 Ws and an H). 2. Once you have done this you write one sentence in Subject-Verb-Object pattern containing some of the 5 Ws and an H. We can also mention the source of information. Examples: Rajesh Singh, MP, was shot dead by unidentified assailants in Jaipur on Thursday, police said.

Prime Minister Narendra Modi flagged off the new bullet train from Mumbai on Saturday.

A sentence in SVO pattern is easy to understand. Unless you are writing an editorial or opinion piece, you can write most of the sentences of the news story in the subject-verb-object pattern.

After writing the intro, you can give the details in the paragraphs below it. The more important information is mentioned in the first few paragraphs and the less important details lower down the story. This is known as the inverted pyramid style of writing. You can visualise an upside-down pyramid with the broad base at the top and the narrow peak at the bottom. In other words, the important information comes at the top. The advantage of writing in this fashion is that a busy reader can read just the first few paragraphs and still get the key information. She can read the rest of the paragraphs if time is available.

You ideally have a quote from the person or persons who gave the key information. This can come in the second or third paragraph. To identify a person, you can mention name, age, address or designation, and organisation or party.

It is better to use short sentences, short paragraphs, simple words and simple sentence structures. Prefer the active voice (write "Rohit ate the biscuit" instead of "The biscuit was eaten by Rohit"). When you use the active voice, it is easy to know who is the doer of the action. This is important for writing news stories. You should cut out fluff or unnecessary words in the sentence. If you can remove a word from a sentence without changing the meaning, then you ought to remove it. You should also avoid jargon which is used by doctors, scientists, etc and replace it with words in simple English.

What is news? My favourite definition of what is news is given in Prof KM Shrivastava's book: "News is an account of a recent event or opinion that is important or interesting." Others have defined it in different ways. News is something based on facts that people would like to read or watch. Hard news is news about something that affects the lives of people. Such news is the most important. Examples: The election of a new government, an earthquake, the appreciation in the value of the rupee. Soft news is interesting to read but does not affect the lives of people. Examples: A story about the wedding ceremony of a film star.

Gathering news: There are several sources of news such as a press statement, a press conference, a speech, or an interview. A reporter may also go to the spot, talk to people and gather information about an incident.

For an interview, the reporter does some homework by reading about the person and prepares a few questions which she can ask. Such questions should be open ended and not close-ended. An open-ended question does not have a one word or yes or no answer. It would be difficult to write a story if the journalist asks only closed-ended questions. A journalist does not prepare all the questions beforehand. The best journalists ask further questions based on what the person says. It is better not to offend or interrupt the person when he or she is speaking. One must be polite at all times. Many journalists record what the person is saying while others take notes of the main points. Some of them write down that they heard after the interview is over but this can be risky. Sometimes interviews are done by sending a set of questions via email. This method is valuable for interviewing experts. Many interviews are done over Zoom, Teams, or Google Meet. If you know the person, you could ask questions over the phone and note down the replies. Whenever possible, face to face interviews give the best results. At first ask a simple question or indulge in small talk to make the person feel comfortable. Then when the interviewee has opened up and started talking, ask more difficult questions. Reveal a little about yourself but not too much, otherwise he will start interviewing you. The interviewee and not the interviewer should be in the spotlight.

A reporter tries to befriend say 50 people in the beat or field which is assigned to him. He stays in touch with them, meets them or talks to them on the phone and asks if they have any news. Sometimes these persons himself inform him when there is news. He gets the basic information and using the knowledge he has about the subject and the background, he writes his news story.

8. b. The experience of reporting

One of the ways in which journalists and writers gather information for their writing is putting questions to people or having conversations.

Before meeting the person, you can think of three or four questions which you are going to ask. You could read about the person or the subject on the internet.

If you are writing about a speech, it would be useful to record it or take notes in a pad. You can then see what is the most important or interesting information in the speech and make that your first paragraph and headline. You can put the rest of the material below it. Later you can rewrite the headline and the first paragraph if you are not satisfied with them.

While talking to people to gather information, it is better to collect a little more information than you need so that you can leave out the dull bits. Otherwise, you might run short of material.

Sometimes you can get material for your writing not by talking to political or business leaders or celebrities but by having conversations with ordinary people. Nobel laureate VS Naipaul wrote several books based on his travels to different parts of the world. He said there was no spokesman or leader he felt compelled to interview. When he went to a country, he tried to speak to many people and then narrow the list to a few whom he could interview at length. He encouraged a person to talk about himself or herself and listened, taking notes if the interviewee did not feel uncomfortable about it. He said he got an understanding of the country from the ordinary people he talked to and got to like. He wrote about these people. Based on life stories of say 20 or 30 people, he drew a profile of the country he was visiting.

While asking questions, first we can ask a simple question which is easy to answer to break the ice. Such questions are called ritual questions. Then once the person starts talking, we can ask open-ended questions. This would encourage the person to talk. We should not interrupt when she is speaking. Quite often it is better not to ask only those questions which we have prepared beforehand but to think of questions based on what the person is saying. At the beginning it is necessary to win the trust of the person so that she feels assured that you are not going to use the information against her.

During a face-to-face interview or video call, we can note facial expressions. Then we will know whether the person is feeling comfortable, whether he would like to continue speaking or you should put the next question.

Television reporters too gather sound bytes in this fashion. A journalist goes with a cameraman to the press conference or the place of the interview. She thinks of four or five questions beforehand. She has to ensure that the person feels comfortable and opens up. Reporters need to be familiar with the news so that they do not feel lost during the interview.

The journalist's task is easier if there is a press release or statement from the political leader, company, police or NGOs. She can skim through the report, find out the most important or interesting or newsworthy point and make this her first paragraph and headline. She can then compose as many paragraphs from the statement as she needs. She needs to attribute the information to the source of the press statement a few times in the write up.

In summary, we can say that a writer or journalist writes on the basis of a written statement or a conversation or his or her own independent thinking.

8. c. What Rohit learnt at a students' newspaper

For a few years, Rohit worked for a students' newspaper in New Delhi and wrote down his experiences.

Some people think that working for a students' newspaper would not enrich one professionally as much as a newspaper for adults, but this is not always the case. Writing and editing for the students' newspaper requires concentration, effort and thought. We have to select material that would be interesting to children and write in a simple, clear way. The students' newspaper helps shape the minds of youngsters. So, our efforts are socially useful and do not go waste, Rohit realised.

Rohit sometimes wrote articles after talking to students or getting their inputs on WhatsApp or email. For selecting the subject, he thought of 10-15 questions which he could ask students. He would get one of these subjects approved by seniors.

Once the subject was selected, he thought of two or three questions which he would put to each student. He sent these on WhatsApp, asking them to send their replies in 100 or 150 words mentioning their names, class, school. Sometimes he asked these questions on the phone and noted down the replies. He tried not to interrupt while they were speaking. After getting all the replies, he would write two introductory paras and then put together the article using the replies of students.

Rohit sometimes wrote articles using material from the internet. He would first search for three websites on Google from where he could get information. He copied this onto a Word file via Notepad. He would skim through the entire material, making those parts bold which he wanted to retain. The points he underlined were those which he found interesting or important and he understood clearly. He would then begin composing paragraphs in his own words using this material. He thought of several headlines and selected one. He did not forget to give credit to the websites from which he had got material.

Rohit once went to cover a literacy project. He carried a notebook and two pens. He thought of two or three questions he would put to the students. In a friendly way, he encouraged the students to talk and listened without interruption. He also spoke to the principal.

On another occasion, Rohit went to cover an essay writing contest. He listened to the speakers and noted down points which he found interesting or useful. He put a few questions to director of the organisation when he met her. He spoke to students and teachers and in addition to their replies to questions, noted down their names, class or designation. These events were simple to cover and are mentioned here to help us understand the basics.

It is more difficult to investigate scams and scandals. The journalist tries to find out the different factions in an organisation and those who are opposed to the ruling group. They befriend the group which is opposed to the ruling faction and try to get some information. Unlike the police, they cannot use force to draw out information. They have to cajole or persuade or outwit the interviewee to get information. The investigation process can also be risky.

8. d. On reading the news

Though Rohit does not spend much time in reading the news and is not an expert, he has given some thought to the subject of reading news.

He reads all the headlines on the BBC App or the app of a daily newspaper once a day. If a news report interests him, he reads a few paras or the entire story.

As he makes a living as a journalist, he cannot afford to follow thinker Rolf Dobelli's advice of not reading the news. He needs to be familiar with the important news items so that he can edit reports on those subjects.

The Dalai Lama listens to the news on the BBC while having breakfast. Later in the day he reads newspapers and newsmagazines. At night he watches BBC TV. Some spiritual leaders feel that news is about worldly matters and tends to focus on the negative side so spiritual aspirants should avoid news. But the Dalai Lama reads the news even though he is a spiritual person.

It does not take much time to skim through the headlines on the BBC App in English or one of the regional languages. It gives only the important developments and explains the hows and whys. It is an analysis with a bit of interpretation which helps the reader understand the news better. In particular, Rohit reads news reports that help him to understand how society and the political system function. He finds the process is enjoyable. But if possible, he avoids reading or watching news during the first two hours after waking up. Reading negative news early in the morning can sometimes spoil the day.

When important developments occur, Rohit reads about them on two news sites. One of them could be critical of the authorities and the other pro-government. Then he gets a balanced picture. It would, however, be best to read about the development from two credible news organisations.

Many young people also like to read about the day's developments on Google News. One of the advantages of this is that you can compare the reporting on the same event by different news organisations. Other youngsters like to get their news from X, formerly Twitter. They follow the work of a few journalists they respect and try to read what they post on X.

* * * * *

9.

Worldly Success, Spiritual Evolution and the Life of Our Dreams

Worldly success as well as spiritual growth—The best practices of Pranab Mukherjee—On daily routines—Our contribution to society and an adequate income—Rohit's simple philosophy of work—On managing work

9. a. Worldly success as well as spiritual growth

We sometimes think that there is a conflict between attaining worldly success and ensuring our spiritual growth. This may be true to some extent, but by following certain guidelines we can achieve both.

Self-help writer Robin gives some guidelines for attaining worldly success and personal growth in the chapter Under the Kimono in his book 'The Greatness Guide'. We can compare and contrast these guidelines with the suggestions made by Swami Sivananda and Mahatma Gandhi for achieving spiritual growth as well as fulfilling our worldly duties.

Both suggest that we wake up early and spend some time for self-development. Robin Sharma suggests that we spend an hour on activities such as physical exercise, journal writing, and reading good books. Swami Sivananda suggests we begin the day with japa and meditation and pranayama, then do yoga asanas or go for a morning walk.

Robin Sharma says we can have five workouts at the gym every week. Mahatma Gandhi suggested that we go for walks daily. It does not matter what form of exercise we take so long as we are regular.

Robin Sharma says we should have a world class diet. Yoga gurus suggest that we have a vegetarian diet that includes milk and milk products and plenty of fruits.

Both suggest that we keep a journal for personal and spiritual growth. We can write in our journal almost daily.

Robin Sharma suggests that we have at least one conversation with an interesting person every week. This would keep our enthusiasm high. Yoga gurus advise use to avoid unnecessary talking and observe silence for one or two hours daily. Spiritual gurus too suggest that we should spend some time in the company of the wise.

Both suggest that we read good books regularly. In addition to these points, Swami Sivananda stresses on spending some time on japa or meditation daily. He also says that if we want rapid spiritual growth, we should try to strive for brahmacharya or celibacy. We also need to control anger. We can stay silent when we become angry or if we are very angry, we can leave the place at once.

In conclusion, we can say that the guidelines for worldly success and spiritual growth are not totally different. For achieving both these goals, we need to pay attention to diet and exercise, keep a journal, avoid talkativeness, and read good books. But of course, for spiritual growth, we need to focus on spiritual books and avoid long chat sessions and acquiring a large number of friends. We need to spend some time alone daily for inner development.

The point is not to think that that the two goals are contradictory but begin by living with a sense of purpose and self-discipline.

9. b. The best practices of Pranab Mukherjee

Late Indian President Pranab Mukherjee (1935 to 2020) did three things almost daily that enabled him to perform at his peak. He went for morning walks, did pooja (prayer), and wrote in his diary daily.

Learning from his example, we can incorporate these activities in our daily routine. When we are disinclined to go for a walk, we can try not to miss it. Instead of pooja or prayer, we might wish to do meditation and the benefits would be similar. The late President wrote one page in his diary each night, reflecting on his life, activities and reading. It is an excellent practice we can follow.

His other interests were reading, gardening and music. He had a collection of books and liked to go through them in his leisure time.

He was awarded India's highest civilian honour the Bharat Ratna in 2019. Anyone who aspires to grow spiritually and intellectually and also do public service can take up these activities: Morning walk, pooja, reading and diary writing.

9. c. On daily routines

If you wish to understand what kind of life a man or a woman has, try to figure out two things: 1. What does he want or aim for in life? and 2. What is his daily routine? Answers to these two questions will help you to understand his life.

The daily routines of a spiritual leader and a writer are described here as examples.

The Dalai Lama: He is a Buddhist monk, leader of the Tibetan Buddhists and a recipient of the Nobel Peace Prize. His daily routine has several interesting features.

He wakes up early, around 3am, has a shower, and does meditation and prostrations. He goes for a walk around the compound in Dharamsala, Himachal Pradesh, India, but when it is raining, he uses a treadmill. During breakfast he listens to the news.

He then meditates for some more time and reads Buddhist texts for an hour. After that he reads newspapers and magazines. He has an early lunch and, in the afternoon, meets visitors or attends to his work. He has evening tea, but no dinner. At night, he watches the news on TV and also meditates. He goes to bed early as he has to wake up early.

Khushwant Singh (1915 to 2014): At one time, he was probably India's most popular writer. When he was in his 50s and 60s, his routine was something like this. He woke up early using an alarm clock. He prepared tea for his guards and read the newspaper headlines. He then listened to hymns broadcast from the Golden Temple, Amritsar.

After playing tennis in the morning, he had a cold shower and breakfast. He spent the next few hours in writing and reading. He avoided phone calls and visitors in the mornings.

He had a light lunch followed by a 30-minute siesta. He sometimes dipped into books of dirty jokes. He replied to letters and then spent some more time reading and writing. After that he went for a swim. In the evening he had three pegs of whisky. Generally, a mehfil gathered around this time. He spent about 40 minutes on drinking. He often had dinner parties. At night he watched the news on TV and went to bed.

If you aspire to become a writer, a CEO, an artist or a businessman and want to know what kind of life such a person leads, try to find out his or her daily routine.

If you wish to become an artist, you should not think of the name and fame but the fact that you will spend several hours daily on your craft. Ideally, your field of work should be something you like doing.

9. d. Our contribution to society and an adequate income

What can we do to serve society and get an adequate income?

We can try to live an exemplary life, have positive interactions with people and do socially useful work. An exemplary life is one when we try to follow the essential teachings of our religion, not be aggressive, and exercise some self-control.

Positive conversations are those when we listen more and speak less, stay silent when people speak harsh words and offer suggestions which we think would benefit the other person.

Anil has a simple philosophy of work: Do your work sincerely, stay silent or give a brief explanation when seniors criticize you, try to update your skills periodically and leave salary and job security in the hands of the Lord.

He has decided to work as long as his health permits. But when he gets quite old, he can consider lighter options and do freelance work.

He has found that if he gets enough sleep and his digestion is fine, he is free from any pain or discomfort and gets some time for the activities he likes doing, then he can do his work satisfactorily.

Anil is lucky as he found a job that he likes doing to some extent. It is not totally a hobby, but he does not dislike his work. He can spend long hours on it without grumbling. In his case, the work involves writing and editing that he likes. For other people, the work they like could be interacting with others such as a sales manager. The work could be research if the person likes reading and writing and patiently going through books, documents and data. If she enjoys learning new things and interacting with youngsters, she would be happy as a teacher.

Anil has decided that if he loses his job, he would spend some time daily searching for regular or freelance work. He will also spend time learning new skills or reading books and articles. He will try to stay physically and mentally fit. In case of difficulty in finding work or an economic depression, he would be mentally prepared to work for a low salary that just covers his basic expenses. If he perseveres, things will improve over a period. Given a choice, he would like to do work that he likes and is socially useful. He needs to pay attention to staying mentally and physically healthy so that he can work. Anil also tries to avoid extravagance so that he can live a good life even on a modest income.

9. e. Rohit's simple philosophy of work

Rohit has a simple philosophy: Whatever job God gives him, he does his best. His aim is to make a sincere effort. There are areas where he is not proficient, but he tries.

Before we choose a field of work, we should try to find out what we like doing and what we are good at. We can do some self-analysis and also get the opinions of people we respect.

When we face work-related problems, we can get guidance from two quotes. The Gita says: "You have a right to work, but are not entitled to the fruits of action."

The writer Thomas Carlyle said: "Blessed is he who has found his work. Let him ask no other blessedness."

It is indeed a blessing if we can find work that we like. It contributes to our health and wellbeing.

9. f. On managing work

On days when Rohit has to handle the schedule for distribution of work, he bears in mind one sentence: Keep on trying and do total surrender to the Lord. His duty is to coordinate the flow of work. It is like a mail sorter in a post office putting letters in different boxes for different destinations.

He also needs to acknowledge messages from seniors which he receives on email or WhatsApp. Just a few words of acknowledgement are fine.

The only things that are needed are the determination to keep on trying, be calm when difficulties arise and be polite (and if necessary, firm). The basic skill is the ability to decide what is suitable for which person and assign work or forward messages or inputs accordingly.

* * * * *

10.

The Well-being of Spouse and Children

Suggestions for a spiritually inclined couple—A devoted wife—The education of our children—Gandhi on the education of children—Study tips by B Stevenson—A scheme for self-education of youngsters—For better conversations—Listening can revive relationships

10. a. Suggestions for a spiritually inclined couple

Spiritually inclined people are sometimes reluctant to get married thinking that marriage would hinder their spiritual and intellectual pursuits. But if they bear in mind a few points, marriage would not be a hindrance in these activities.

Ramakrishna Paramhamsa said that after the birth of one or two children, the married couple can have celibacy as their ideal. Swami Sivananda said that even married couples should restrict physical indulgence and after the age of 40, have brahmacharya or celibacy as the ideal. They might fail occasionally, but they should keep striving for it. In other words, the marital relationship should be less carnal and more spiritual.

We need to do a moderate amount of socially useful work. If we choose to get married, it is our duty to do some paid work to ensure financial survival, unless we have some other source of income. We can also help in household work even if that is monotonous.

We must find time for our family. We can try to listen when our partner speaks without interrupting and try not to speak harsh words. When an argument seems to be developing, we can try to stay silent. It is better not to be too critical of one's spouse. One must think twice before pointing out weaknesses. A word of genuine appreciation can rejuvenate the relationship.

If we are on the spiritual path, we can observe certain spiritual disciplines. These disciplines would depend on our religion, but everyone can avoid illicit sex or adultery, alcohol and tobacco. We might consider becoming a vegetarian. We can also avoid extravagance so as not to affect the monthly budget. We can pray for our spouse, children and parents.

There is some truth in the saying that marriages are made in heaven. There is a lasting bond between the husband and wife, but it is also necessary to allow our partner to have some space and time for solitary pursuits such as reading or meditation. There is such a thing as too much togetherness. Kahlil Gibran said, "You were born together, and together you shall be forevermore…But let there be spaces in your togetherness…Sing and dance together and be joyous, but let each one of you be alone...And stand together yet not too near together."

10. b. A devoted wife

She begins her day with a bath and pooja or prayers for herself and her family. For the main prayers, she does not need to refer to religious texts. When she has doubts, she consults a pandit. What is needed in prayer is sincerity and the method is not too important for Ramakrishna Paramhamsa said, "Pray in any way you like, for God hears even the footfall of an ant." When they see her, her husband and son get the feeling that the blessings of the Lord are with the family.

She also does pranayama and physical exercises in the mornings. Her morning walk gets neglected when there is a lot of household work. After doing some household work in the mornings, she has a plate of fruits.

It is good that she avoids unnecessary phone calls during the first two hours of the morning to focus. When her husband or son is ill, she pays extra attention to them.

She rests for a while after lunch. In the afternoons she gives private tuitions which allows her to use her mental abilities for the benefit of others. She also teaches some poor students free.

Outside the home, she is bold and assertive. Her family members get worried that she will get involved in quarrels.

Earlier, she used to love reading English and Hindi literature and had read the works of several good writers. These books taught her how to live a good life and built her character. Unfortunately, the reading habit became less important after marriage. At the end of a busy day when she is exhausted, she sometimes watches television serials and YouTube videos.

It is said that God rewards a sincere spiritual aspirant with a good wife. This thought sometimes occurs to her husband, making him happy.

10. c. The education of our children

If we decide to get married and have children, it is our duty and also a privilege to educate them.

A basic thing we can do is talk to the child regularly and after listening to him for a while, offer suggestions that we think will benefit him.

While in conversation, you can try not to get angry. If you find that you are getting irritated or angry, you can stay silent. Or if negative thoughts arise, you can silently repeat a mantra a few times. Listening is the key, and it is better not to thrust your ideas on the child.

You can encourage him to read his textbooks and books of general interest. He can also do online courses and watch good videos. If so inclined, he can solve Maths problems regularly.

You can encourage him to go for walks or play games regularly. The child must consume an adequate amount of fruits and milk.

You can encourage the child to write in his or her journal writing at least once a week. If she is old enough, she can do mindful meditation.

Once in a while, you can remind him about the moral code of your religion such as the Buddhist Panchashil: Do not kill, steal, indulge in sensuality, tell lies or take intoxicants.

A child needs a few friends, but it is better to avoid long periods of idle talk.

Will the child survive in this world? Yes, he can if he stays healthy, follows the essential teachings of religion, is able to think for himself, has the habit of working and can interact with others positively.

10. d. Gandhi on the education of children

Mahatma Gandhi was not satisfied with the existing education system. He has written several chapters on the subject in his autobiography. You can skim through these when you think about the education of children.

At the farm in South Africa which Gandhi had set up, inmates or outside teachers taught different subjects. Working on the farm gave children physical exercise. For spiritual education, Gandhi taught the basic principles of religion and relied mainly on personal contact. He used to teach the children through conversations. Children remember what they have heard from teachers more easily than what they have read in books, he said.

10. e. Study tips by B Stevenson

Here are some guidelines for youngsters on how to study based on the book 'How to Pass Exams' by B Stevenson and some other books. She says you can study best if you have a room to yourself. Some students can study well in a library where the presence of others studying motivates them. But you can go to a library only if there is one nearby.

If you want to concentrate, there should not be any noise in the background. It is wrong to think that you can study well if the television or radio is playing in the room.

It is difficult to study after a heavy meal. Ideally you should have one sitting on an empty stomach and then study sometime after the meal. The best time to study is in the morning but you can make use of this time only if you do not have to go to school or college. If you try to study lying down in bed, you are likely to fall asleep.

You can have 30-minute periods of reading. But if you are writing or preparing notes, you can study for about an hour at a stretch and then take a short break. After reading for say 30 minutes, you can try to write down whatever you can recall in your notebook. This will help you to think over the material, understand it better, and commit it to memory. After studying something today, you can go through it again the next day and then once before the exams. This way the content will be etched in your mind.

How would you select a book for studying? Skim through the back and front cover and the contents. If necessary, glance through one or two pages. You will get an idea what kind of book it is and whether you will understand and perhaps enjoy it.

You can spend some time on reading news on a website. Good news websites contain news, comment and a little entertainment.

If you have leisure, you can also visit exhibitions and attend public lectures. Then you can watch selected television programmes. But one must not spend too much time on television as it can destroy concentration and waste time. You will gain from television only if you are selective in what you watch.

If you cannot cope with some subjects like Maths or foreign languages, it would be better to get a private tutor. It might consume a lot of time if you try to study on your own or you might also get stuck in some places. In case you cannot get a tutor, you can get a book which is designed for self-study and study the solved examples. Once you have understood them, you can attempt the simpler exercises.

10. f. A scheme for self-education of youngsters

What should a young adult who has not got adequate opportunities for education do to educate herself by her own efforts?

The youngster can take steps to stay healthy: go for walks, do physical exercises or play games. She must include milk and fruits in her diet and try to avoid smoking, drinking or drugs.

She needs to study her textbooks, general interest books and articles on her own initiative. She can keep a journal, writing down her thoughts and feelings several times a week.

For spiritual development, she can follow the essential teachings of her religion. She can pray and perhaps learn to meditate and do it for 10 minutes daily.

She can try to do something that requires concentration in the morning. This will make it easier for her to focus on her studies later in the day. It is better to avoid social media during the first two hours after waking up. Though she has to rely mainly on self-education, she can try to find one or two wise women or men whom she can meet for conversations from time to time. She also needs to make two or three like-minded friends.

Sexual desires are strong in late teens and early 20s, but the youngsters are usually not mentally and emotionally mature to have sexual relationships. Psychologists say that masturbation is a healthy outlet for boys and girls.

The youngster can enrol at an open school or university and sit for exams to get certificates. For learning skills such as English grammar, algebra or calculus, she can take private tuition. The role of the parents, brothers and sisters is to motivate the youngster to sit down to study regularly and follow some kind of daily routine. The parents should see that the youngster does not get demoralised and stop making efforts.

We learn the important things in life by our own efforts. Other people can guide us or motivate us, but most of the learning has to be done by ourselves. Consider two quotes on self-education.

Oscar Wilde said, "Education is an admirable thing but it is well to remember from time to time that nothing that is worth knowing can be taught."

Isaac Asimov said, "Self-education is, I firmly believe, the only kind of education there is."

What does this imply? We should encourage youngsters to find things out and learn on their own and we can only facilitate the process. We can motivate the youngster to make an effort to learn. Once the child gets into the habit of reading, writing, solving maths problems, handling a computer, and likes the process, he or she is already on the path of educating himself or herself.

10. g. For better conversations

Sometimes, a spiritually inclined person needs to socialize though she would prefer to meditate, read or just rest. How can she have useful conversations at such times?

She must try to be polite at all times. Do not say anything to hurt the feelings of the other person. There is no need to criticize or speak harsh words. Accept and appreciate the person as he or she is.

Ask open-ended questions (questions which cannot be answered with just a 'yes' or a 'no' and need a longer answer.) If you just listen with interest, the person will gradually open up and start speaking. You can ask about the person's daily routine, what she likes to do in her free time and off day and what she plans to do in future.

If the person says something you dislike or do not agree with, avoid arguments and just listen but try to change the topic.

You can listen more and speak less. Do not reveal your innermost thoughts. If you talk in this way, you will not lose your inward concentration. Avoid talking loosely about sex with members of the opposite sex.

You can ask questions about topics about which you want to learn or are interested in. Suppose some problem is troubling you. You can ask questions based on that in general terms and will be able to learn from the person. Ralph Waldo Emerson said, "Do you know the secret of the true scholar? Every man is my superior in some way. In that I can learn of him."

Listening with empathy is the key to the success of the interaction. But make sure you do not criticise.

In office, talkativeness can destroy concentration. Sometimes you might be tempted to say something, but try to avoid talkativeness.

Remember, a spiritual person's role is mainly to ask questions and listen with goodwill. After listening for a while, if you think it is right, you can offer suggestions which you think would benefit her or him. Even if you do not offer suggestions, it is important not to say anything negative. Do not say anything out of animosity.

10. h. Listening can revive relationships

People have a desire to be understood and appreciated, but significant people in their lives may not care to listen to them. While one person is speaking, instead of listening attentively, the other may be thinking of what to say next and formulating his responses, according to noted self-help writer Robin Sharma. To have a good conversation, we need to listen twice much as we speak and try not to interrupt while the other person is speaking, Sharma adds.

When we want to learn from other people, say a mentor, a counsellor or a senior colleague, we can write down a few questions beforehand and then ask them. All the questions need not be thought of beforehand. It is best to ask further questions on the basis of what the other person has said. If we think of too many questions beforehand and don't ask any based on what the person has said, then the conversation is likely to become mechanical. We can ask questions about things we want to learn. By having conversations, we can learn not only from experts, but also from those with little formal education. People who have studied only for a few years in schools can sometimes give useful insights. When we are trying to learn from other people, we can take notes. Or perhaps if the other person has no objection, we can record the conversation on our phones.

If we listen attentively without interrupting, the other person would like to continue speaking. Summarise what the person has said in a few words to indicate that you are listening and would like her to go on.

Swami Sivananda suggests that even busy people should try to observe silence for one hour daily. Unnecessary talking drains our mental energy and makes it difficult to focus.

The great yogi suggested that if we cannot avoid talking, we should cut down on all long and unnecessary talk. Friends who come for idle talk can be a hindrance in spiritual pursuits.

A word of caution. Khushwant Singh has written about compulsive talkers. They are on the lookout for a person who can listen to their monologues. They can speak for an hour without giving you a chance to say anything. If you detect such a person, Singh suggested that you avoid him. Khushwant Singh liked the pleasures of life, but he said he avoided gup shup or long gossip sessions with friends.

According to the philosopher Jiddu Krishnamurti, listening to someone with empathy without thinking hard is a form of love. If we want to improve a relationship, the first step can be to listen to the person when she is speaking. Do not think hard and just be present in the moment without thinking of your response. For this reason, theologian Paul Tillich said, "The first duty of love is to listen."

* * * * *

11.

The Wisdom of Tolstoy, Gibran, Khushwant Singh, Dr Chopra, Krishnamurti

Should Anil become a monk?—The intuitive wisdom of Kahlil Gibran—Views of Khushwant Singh on religion—Dr Deepak Chopra on finding joy in life—Krishnamurti on knowledge and education

11. a. Should Anil become a monk?

A young man or woman who is contemplating whether they should become a monk or take up a job and get married would benefit from reading Russian writer Leo Tolstoy's novella 'Father Sergius'.

In the novella, when his fiancée tells Stephen Kasatsky that she has loved before, he is unable to come to terms with it. On learning that her lover was the Emperor, he decides to become a monk.

He lives as a hermit in a cell away from the city. A young, wealthy widow places a bet with her friends that she would test the self-control of Stephen or Father Sergius as he is now known. She goes to his cell at night. Father Sergius realizes that lust is arising in his mind which is overwhelming. She pleads from outside. He starts praying and when he is still unable to control himself, he picks up an axe and chops off a part of his little finger so that the pain can help him conquer lust. When the woman realizes what he has done, she decides to repent and becomes a nun.

One day a woman requests Father Sergius to lay his hands on the head of his son who is ill. He gets cured. The fame of Father Sergius grows and many people start visiting him to discuss their worldly problems or get sick people cured. He continues his routine of prayer, Bible reading, simple food and conversations with visitors. This continues for some years.

Owing to the large number of visitors, he does not get enough time for solitude and prayer. His spiritual strength weakens.

One day a merchant brings his daughter who is ill and requests Father Sergius to bless her. When the young woman is alone with Father Sergius, she says she had seen him in a dream, takes his hand in hers and places it on her breasts. Finding that desire has gone out of control, Father Sergius yields.

When he realizes what he has done, he runs away from his cell in peasant clothes. He goes to the house of a girl he had known in his childhood whom her friends considered foolish. He finds that she is working and looking after her family.

He then finds employment with a well-to-do peasant. He works on a farm, teaches children and nurses the sick. He realizes the importance of work and love in life. In another book, Tolstoy writes, “Life can be lived magnificently if one knows how to work and how to love.”

11. b. The intuitive wisdom of Kahlil Gibran

Some chapters in Kahlil Gibran’s ‘The Prophet’ can be read again and again, in particular the ones on marriage, children, work, self-knowledge, teaching, pain and death. You can read one or two of these small chapters after finishing the day’s work.

Gibran has said several wise things about self-knowledge and teaching. About self-knowledge he said, “Your hearts know in silence the secrets of the days and the nights/ But your ears thirst for the sound of your heart’s knowledge. You would know in words what you have always known in thought.”

On teaching he said, “No man can reveal to you aught but (anything except) that which already lies half asleep in the dawning of your knowledge. The teacher who walks in the shadow of the temple, among his followers, gives not of his wisdom, but rather of his faith and his lovingness.”

These sentences can guide us when we are teaching people through conversation. We can teach only those things of which the other person has a rough understanding. She can understand what we are saying only if she already has a rough idea about it in her mind. We can encourage the person to talk about himself and listen. This will enable us to understand her thoughts and feelings. Then we can tell her things which we think she will understand.

As far as our own education is concerned, we need not read too much after a certain age. We can know things by thinking and using our powers of intuition. We should keep ourselves busy in something that requires concentration, effort and thought. This will assist our mental growth.

On marriage he says that the husband and wife shall be together even after death in some form. But while they are on the planet, there should be spaces in their togetherness. Regarding children, he said that we should give children our love and not thrust our thoughts on them.

We can use Gibran's wisdom about children, self-knowledge and teaching to impart knowledge to youngsters. A child has to be mentally ready to receive this wisdom.

He needs to be mentally active by doing reading, journal writing, or any other work that requires thought and concentration. We should encourage him to talk about himself and must not interrupt. Then we can offer suggestions that we think will benefit him. Those ideas that are not yet fully formed in the youngster's mind would be reinforced and developed by the conversation. We should show love and kindness and encourage him to learn by his own efforts.

11. c. Views of Khushwant Singh on religion

Khushwant Singh had the public image of a man fond of wine and women, but he had read scriptures of different religions and given thought to them, so his views on religion deserve consideration.

He said in the religion he had devised for himself, God had no place. He gave reasons for this. He felt that injustice often prevailed in the world. Spastic or blind children were sometimes born to good parents. Sometimes children died young and God did not prevent this, he said.

As for the founders of religion, we should think of them as human beings with extraordinary abilities. They had the power to influence large numbers of people. But they had several human weaknesses. Despite these factors, many people can tolerate criticism of God, but they grow violent when someone talks ill of the founder of their religion.

Regarding the scriptures of different religions, he said he preferred reading the classics of literature to the scriptures. The scriptures are generally in ancient languages which people do not understand fully. People chant or recite the scriptures instead of reading them as works of religious philosophy. In such a situation what should we do? We can read works on spirituality and religious philosophy by modern writers whom we respect in addition to the scriptures. Leo Tolstoy had written that he was saved by some contemporary religious writers.

Khushwant Singh felt that places of worship had become centres of commerce from where priests and purohits drew their sustenance. The best place for worship is our home, he said.

Religions stress on prayer, telling the beads or meditation, but Singh felt that these activities were a waste of time. He said people who mediate do so to get peace of mind, but he asked them what does peace of mind give? Khushwant Singh said that great works of science or literature were often produced by restless or disturbed minds, and peace of mind was a sterile concept. He said meditation could be a therapy for hypertension or for disturbed minds, but was otherwise not necessary. I think many people would disagree with him.

Khushwant Singh said that religions were products of their times. They were devised to suit the social and economic conditions of the time they were born. They cannot be considered to hold true at all times.

He said the only religious principle he subscribed to was non-violence or ahimsa. As the Jains say, ahimsa paramo dharma or non-violence is the highest religion.

We may or may not agree with Singh's views, but his ideas provide an intellectual framework for thinking and subjecting our religious practices to scrutiny.

11. d. Dr Deepak Chopra on finding joy in life

Renowned self-help writer and medical practitioner Dr Deepak Chopra has mentioned some ways of finding joy in life in his book 'Overcoming Addiction'. He mentions a set of points which we can discuss here.

The first thing for finding happiness in life is that you should try to get enough sleep. If you sleep for less than six hours or more than 10 hours at night, then this is probably an area that needs adjustments.

You should try to begin the day with nurturing activities. The first few hours of the day need to be spent wisely. Mornings are an excellent time to meditate. There is no need to watch the news or other programmes on television just after waking up as they often contain negative information that can make you start the day on a bad note. He says that according to Ayurveda, the ancient Indian science of health, you should have a light or no breakfast.

Also ask yourself whether you are getting satisfaction from your work. If you get a good salary, but hate your work, it would hamper your enjoyment of life.

You can also ask yourself whether you are able to express anger in a constructive way. Dr Chopra says that it can often be damaging to express your anger suddenly, but it is also harmful to let it fester within. We ought to express anger constructively in ways that do not harm others or ourselves. Instead of expressing anger suddenly, we should first "digest" it and then express it to the person who annoyed us.

To find happiness, you should spend some time daily on activities you enjoy. You can also spend some time in solitude. Having some quiet time with ourselves helps us regain our peace and recharge our mind.

You might like to spend some time in the midst of nature. Go for a walk in a park or sit near a water body. If that is not possible, take care of a potted plant in your flat.

It sounds obvious but we tend to forget this: Rest for a while when you get tired. Don't try to accomplish a lot in a hurry. The world will not collapse if you rest for a while.

And finally, show love to your family members and friends and receive their love in return. Talking, listening, sharing a meal together or going for a walk together are some simple ways of expressing love.

11. e. Krishnamurti on knowledge and education

Spiritual philosopher Jiddu Krishnamurti says that the aim of education is to develop an integrated individual and not just increase intellectual abilities. The individual should be able to think for himself and not be violent.

The teacher does not need degrees to teach, but should have a passion for teaching. He does not need to learn a method, a system; if he is keen to teach, he will develop his own method of teaching.

The problem in education is the educator (parents and teachers) and not the child. The educator needs to observe the child and teach accordingly. He cannot have one method for all children.

If parents and teachers are themselves not able to control passion, they cannot teach self-control to children. They need to sort their problems first.

Krishnamurti says we need to observe ourselves: our thoughts, feelings and desires. Self-observation will enable us to understand ourselves. This is the first step and the next is to have love and compassion.

What we need is a psychological transformation of the individual. A violent social revolution will not improve the world. It will replace one set of oppressors with another, said Krishnamurti.

Krishnamurti says that truth is a pathless land. One cannot come to it through any organised religion or sect.

When Anil looks back, he feels happy that he did not become a full-time member of any religious organisation. Then he would not have had intellectual freedom. He would not be free to experiment and find out the truth and would have had to follow the rules prescribed by the organisation.

Moreover, when he was young, he was not mentally prepared for brahmacharya or celibacy. He would not have been happy in the organisation.

* * * * *

12.

Restful Sleep and Working All Night

How to get restful sleep—Sleep and spiritual practices

12. a. How to get restful sleep

Adequate sleep is necessary to function efficiently and be mentally healthy. Here are some tips on how we can get sound sleep.

We can go for walks in the daytime or be physically active to facilitate sound sleep at night. This is especially important for those who do brain work for a living. Brain workers may find it hard to get sound sleep if they do not do physical exercises or go for walks.

We can avoid sleeping in the daytime. If at all we wish to sleep, we can avoid sleeping for more than 30 or 40 minutes in the daytime. This rule is obviously not applicable to those who do night duty.

We can avoid tea and coffee in the evening and night. We can also avoid intense brain work close to bedtime such as filing income tax returns or reading an exciting novel.

At bedtime if we cannot fall asleep, we can sit on the bed or in a chair and repeat mantras till we feel sleepy. If we are not mentally exhausted, we can do light reading.

If worries prevent us from falling asleep, we can write down what we are worried about and what we can do about it the next morning. Once we define the problem and have a method of tackling it, it will seem less threatening. When we get into bed, we can try to do total surrender to the Lord, leaving our problems and worries in His hands. If needed, we can sit on the bed and pray.

If we cannot fall asleep, we can just lie down, close our eyes and relax. This will also relax our body and mind and after a while we might fall sleep.

It is better to avoid sleeping pills and alcohol to fall asleep. But in case we have an important assignment the next morning and cannot fall asleep, we can consider having a pill. Pills should be taken occasionally, if at all on the advice of a doctor. Psychiatrists prescribe sleeping pills to those whose sleep has been disturbed for quite some time so that sleep patterns improve.

12. b. Sleep and spiritual practices

Anil, a man in 50s, asked himself what keeps him in a sound mental state and he arrived at this answer.

He found from experience that if he gets five to six hours of sleep and is able to do his spiritual practices for about 60 minutes, then he is in a sound mental state. His morning routine consists of japa or mantra meditation, walking or physical exercises and journal writing. In addition to these he tries to keep his mind free from sensual thoughts. After finishing his morning routine, he makes a resolution to keep on trying all day.

Sleep: At bedtime, if he cannot fall asleep he looks at photos on a site such as Magnum Photos or reads a little but avoids intense mental work. He has found that if he goes for a walk in the daytime, he gets better sleep at night.

Japa: He does chanting or japa for 20 to 30 minutes every morning just after waking up and brushing his teeth. He does more japa later in the day whenever he gets some free time.

Journal writing: He has found from experience that writing down his thoughts and feelings for 20 minutes or more keeps him mentally healthy. All that is bottled up inside him comes out. He feels better after emptying his mind. There is much truth in the words of Lord Byron, "If I don't write to empty my mind, I go mad."

Walking: He usually goes for a walk just after his meditation but before his journal writing. After writing one tends to feel disinclined to step out of the house so he goes for a walk before he begins writing. Walking relaxes and soothes the mind, put him in a thinking mode and also makes him physically active.

Night duty: From time to time Anil has to do night duty in office. The main challenge he faces is how to get enough sleep in the daytime. If he cannot fall asleep in the daytime, he goes for a short walk and does mantra meditation lying down in bed without a rosary. He tells himself that he should try to give rest to his mind and body even if he does not get enough sleep. After getting a few hours of sleep, he generally does freewriting, that is, writes down whatever comes to mind till two to three pages are filled up. He just pours out what he is feeling without making an effort to write well.

When his colleague Arjun has night duty, he tries to get the basic minimum amount of sleep every 24 hours.

While returning home in the Metro train in the morning, he does 15 minutes of manasic japa or mental repetition of mantras. When he returns home after work, he has a glass of warm milk with Horlicks and repeats a mantra till he falls asleep even though he is distracted by various thoughts. He tries to rest even if he cannot fall asleep. If he is too worried, he just lies down in bed or sits in a chair and does nothing for a while.

To reduce mental fatigue, he climbs stairs or goes for a walk. Despite all these efforts if he cannot fall asleep, he takes a sleeping pill which a psychiatrist has advised.

He avoids too many cups of tea at night. Caffeine drives away sleep.

If he wakes up after sleeping for only a short duration, he avoids looking at the clock. Seeing the time frequently can make a person worried.

Mahatma Gandhi had control over sleep. This means that he could sleep whenever he desired. But this is almost impossible for most people. We can create the right atmosphere and relax, and sleep will come when it has to.

While working in office at night, Anil has found from experience that it is better to have only fruits and not any other heavy food item. During night duty, he has the motto of "Remember God and keep on trying."

* * * * *

13.

The Control and Sublimation of Desire

Controlling desire enables us to achieve lofty goals—Celibacy for householders over 40 years of age—Avoiding heavy meals at night

13. a. Controlling desire enables us to achieve lofty goals

In his book 'Think and Grow Rich,' Napoleon Hill talks about sex transmutation which means that you try not to think about sex and instead think of something higher. Transmutation requires willpower but the reward is worth the effort.

He said that if we turn our thoughts away from physical expression of desire, we may become geniuses. Great writers rely on the still, small voice from within or their intuition. This faculty can be developed by transmutation of desire.

Why should we try to keep our minds free from lust? The reward is great. If our mind is free from desire, we can hear the still, small voice from within and our powers of intuition will develop.

A person who avoids excessive indulgence should not worry when he or she crosses the age of 40 or 50. If our minds are relatively free from lustful thoughts, we can achieve great things in our 50s or even later. Those who succeed in an outstanding way seldom do so before their 40s, says Hill. More often, they do not strike their real pace until they are way beyond their 50s.

Hill does not say that we should give up physical contact totally. But we can try to avoid excessive indulgence.

13. b. Celibacy for householders over 40 years of age

Even a married person who aspires for rapid spiritual development should try to observe brahmacharya or celibacy. Before the age of 40, he can restrict the indulgence. After that age, he can strive for greater control. He may sometimes fail but should keep on trying.

Indulgence is acceptable in the initial years of marriage, but after the birth of one or two children, the couple can exercise some restraint, said the great saint Ramakrishna Paramhamsa.

Having non-vegetarian food, overeating or eating just for taste excite passion, so a spiritual aspirant can try to avoid these.

A spiritual aspirant should try to avoid pornography or talking loosely about sex. When passion troubles him, he can repeat a mantra for a while or pray silently. This will help him to control his mind.

Members of ISKCON say that sex is meant for procreation and not for recreation. Even married devotees aim for brahmacharya after the birth of one or two children.

It is easy to observe brahmacharya if one is convinced about its benefits. Brahmacharya brings about peace of mind and contentment.

Mahatma Gandhi said, "The conquest of lust is the highest endeavour in a man or woman's existence."

Brahmacharya (celibacy) means freedom from sexual desire or abstinence from intercourse. For a married couple, it means restricting the indulgence. It is a help in the spiritual path. The first step is to be convinced about its benefits and then we can keep on trying to observe it.

It is difficult to control passion. We can be successful in a physical sense, but stray lustful thoughts may sometimes arise. When this happens, we can repeat a mantra a few times.

A life of brahmacharya (celibacy) is glorious, but moderation in the household life is equally good. Great rishis in ancient India were married but they did not lead a life of lust, said Swami Sivananda.

Yogis say moderation in household life means indulgence about once a month. After the age of 40 or so, complete brahmacharya can be the ideal.

If we want to observe brahmacharya, we should pay attention to our diet. We must eat to live and not live to eat.

Overeating and eating just for taste makes control difficult. We should try to stay busy most of the time. If our mind is busy in work, reading or japa, lustful thoughts will not arise. We also need to do some physical exercises or go for walks during the daytime. Then the fatigue of the day will produce sound sleep at night.

After checking passion, we will enjoy bliss from within, said Swami Sivananda.

Brahmacharya is freedom from sexual desire. A spiritual aspirant should strive for this ideal state. The view popular today is that controlling desire is unnatural and unhealthy, but several great saints have stressed on the importance of self-control.

It is believed that sexual love and fulfilment are something good. But for spiritual progress, we need to exercise self-control to some extent.

For an unmarried youngster, masturbation is a healthy outlet, say psychologists, but it should not be excessive. A young married person needs to avoid adultery. Stray adulterous thoughts may arise, which he or she has to control. After some years, sexual desires become less intense. Nocturnal emissions may sometimes occur, but they do not cause harm.

13. c. Avoiding heavy meals at night

Some spiritual masters advise us to avoid foodgrain after sunset and have just fruits, vegetables, juices, milk or soups. It is sometimes hard to control the desire to eat tasty things at night as you feel that if you have just fruits, you won't get sound sleep. A middle path would be to have fruits on most days, but when you are mentally exhausted, depressed or under stress, you can have a proper meal. The problem with a heavy meal at night is the possibility of constipation.

At night you can have a glass of water, lie down in bed and do manasic japa (mantra meditation) till your feel sleepy. The desire to have food for pleasure will come and then subside. But if you are genuinely hungry, you might as well have a meal and not criticise myself severely for it.

Gluttony is linked to a lot of other things. For instance, we find that when we talk a lot, we feel like having something tasty to eat.

The Dalai Lama has evening tea but no dinner. One could adopt a middle path and instead of avoiding dinner, have just fruits on most days.

* * * * *

14.

Keep on Trying, Live in the Present, Surrender to God's Will

The importance of trying—The concept of surrender—When everything seems uncertain—Living one day at a time—Coping with evil in the world—When major worldly problems arise

14. a. The importance of trying

On certain days when we need to do a challenging task, but feel we will not succeed, we wish we could get away. We can tell ourselves that all we need to do is to make a sincere attempt. No matter what others might say, we can consider ourselves to be successful in this task as long as we keep on trying.

We need to avoid those things that would weaken our willpower or the determination to keep on trying. Some things that could weaken our resolve are indulging in idle chatter, eating just for pleasure, thinking excessively, reading for too long, or sensuality.

We also need to avoid things that will make us lose our concentration. Idle talk is a major enemy of concentration. We can listen to someone, if necessary, but should avoid speaking too much. We can try to avoid arguments. Otherwise, we would think about the ugly exchange of words for a long time and not be able to focus on our task.

The Buddha realized the importance of effort in the spiritual path. There is no place for the idler in Buddhism. It is wrong to think that Buddhism promotes passivity and inertia. The stress is on striving and not worrying about the outcome. For these reasons, Right Effort is a part of the Buddhist path to salvation, called the Noble Eightfold Path.

When we face obstacles in the spiritual path, Swami Sivananda said that all that is expected from us is sincere effort. The American writer Elbert Hubbard said, "There is no failure except in no longer trying."

The Gita stresses that we need to make an effort without thinking too much about failure or victory. If we adopt this attitude, we would be able to keep on trying and not lose heart. "Fight for the sake of fighting, without thinking about joy or sorrow, loss or gain, victory or defeat," said Lord Krishna.

According to the Gita, the minds of those who are not firm in their resolve consider too many options. They lose their sense of purpose. We need to give up the desire for sensual fulfilment and strive to make progress on our chosen path.

College professors tell their students when they fear failure in a particular subject: "You mustn't give up. Spend an hour on the subject daily."

14. b. The concept of surrender

The principle of surrendering to the will of God means that we follow the essential teachings of our religion, keep on trying, and leave the rest in His hands. God will do what is good for us.

We must not give up and should keep on trying to solve the problem. Our duty is to make an attempt. Surrendering to the will of God does not mean that we stop making an effort but should try to do what we can.

The essential teachings of our religion could be, for instance, the Buddhist Panchashil: Abstain from killing, stealing, unwise sexual behaviour, lying or taking intoxicants. A Christian could follow the commandments and a Muslim the Five Pillars of Islam. All we need to do is to make sure that we do not commit grievous sins. We need to control lust, anger and greed because these three impel us to commit sin.

When a difficult situation arises, a devotee says: "God, I am an instrument in your hands. Let Thy will be done." She ceases to struggle against the inevitable and accepts what happens. God knows what is good for us and will do that.

When hard times come, a devotee does her best and leaves matters in the hands of God. She does not drive herself crazy over what might happen in future.

We may be worried about a hundred things. We can do what we can and leave the rest in His hands.

14. c. When everything seems uncertain

Mahatma Gandhi said, "I think it is wrong to expect certainties in this world where all else except God that is Truth is uncertain."

How do we deal with uncertainties? The essential teachings of religion are more or less constant over time. We can follow them and leave the rest to God.

When we face major problems, we can do japa (remember God) and keep on trying. During our morning meditation and journal writing, we can ask ourselves what we should do on that day. Our intuition will tell us what we need to do. We should try to do the things which are to be done on that day and need not worry about the future. The tasks have to be done in the order of their importance. The most important task has to be given priority.

What are some of the things that could go wrong? Our own health or that of a family member could deteriorate. Or we could face financial problems. What is worse, we or someone in our family could commit a grievous sin.

For instance, if we face uncertainty regarding our job, what can we do? The Gita says: "You have a right to work but are not entitled to the fruits of action." We can make it a point to do our work sincerely and leave job security in the hands of God. It would be better if we stay silent when seniors speak harsh words; if necessary, we can give a brief explanation. If we do not have a job, we can remember God and keep on searching for one and also acquire new skills. During the period when our income is limited, we can adopt the motto of simple living and high thinking.

We must remember that if our health is fine, we can always do some work. So, we must go for walks or take other exercise and have nutritious food.

Swami Sivananda said, "A devotee always says that God does everything and he is an instrument in His hands. Let Thy will, not mine be done." We can remember these words when we fall ill or cannot fall asleep at night.

14. d. Living one day at a time

When we wake up in the morning, we generally have a rough idea of what we want to accomplish on that day. We can write down the important things we plan to do on that day.

We may not be able to do everything we plan to do, but some kind of list ought to be there. Then we can focus on the things that need attention. We can then set about tackling these things even if they do not go as planned due to unexpected developments during the day.

What is important is to focus on the things we need to accomplish today without worrying about the future. If we fear something in the future, we can ask ourselves what we need to do about it today and then make an effort. Thinking too much about the future would make us feel overwhelmed.

Sometimes we feel that the present is bad, and the future would be rosy. So, we tend to put off enjoying the little pleasures today. But we need to find time today for the things we love doing such as a new sport, watching a good movie, or reading the latest book by our favourite author. There is no need to postpone these activities to the future when we think the conditions will be better.

We also tend to have regrets about the way we have lived, the mistakes we have committed in the past. We sit and brood and waste our time. We should try to put a "full stop" to such regrets about the past. Nobody has perfect foresight and people make different kinds of mistakes. We cannot foresee the impact certain actions will have in the future. Because of this we all make mistakes. The important thing is to learn the lessons from the past and not repeat them in future. We must move on.

The present day is important. Instead of thinking too much about the future or the past, we must focus on doing the things we plan to do TODAY.

14. e. Coping with evil in the world

What are the characteristics of a bad environment? The people in authority are driven just by the desire for sex, money and power. They are not interested in the pursuit of knowledge or philanthropy, reading books and consume content with a lot of sex and violence. They tell lies and are verbally aggressive. Silence is like death for them.

In such places, people in positions of power indulge in illicit sex, smoke and drink, and gorge on food. They do not have the motivation to work and are disinclined to make an effort. They may talk about meditation and prayer but do not actually do it.

Harsh words: A form of violence which we experience regularly is the harsh words of people. It is like the sting of a bee on the mind.

We should try to endure harsh words but may give an explanation if necessary. In other words, we can follow the Biblical injunction "Resist not evil." If we silently endure harsh words, God will protect our interests. Enduring verbal aggression in silence will strengthen us mentally and spiritually.

The evil in this world: When we face an evil situation, we should do what we can to overcome it. If nothing can be done, we have to accept it.

Evil gives us an opportunity to make an effort and emerge stronger. Instead of complaining about the situation, we have to face it and the striving will make us stronger and wiser. Evil exists so that we can make an effort to overcome it.

There is evil which we can prevent and evil which we cannot. When we face evil or suffering which we cannot avoid, we have to accept it with fortitude. If we can do something about it, we need to make a constant effort.

It is said that suffering is the father of wisdom. If we face suffering with the right attitude and do what we can, we will grow stronger and wiser.

14. f. When major worldly problems arise

What can a spiritually inclined person do when they face major worldly problems?

We can begin the day with say 20 minutes of spiritual practices such as mantra meditation. The duration can be less than usual. After meditation or prayers, we can face the problem. It would be better to avoid journal writing in the morning on a day when we face a lot of uncertainty and we can write later in the day.

When we get a moment's leisure, we can either do manasic japa (mental repetition of mantras) or try to tackle our problems. We can avoid writing or reading till the work is done or till the evening.

When dealing with people, we need to be polite with everyone. If someone criticizes us, we can try to stay silent.

When we face problems, we must resist the temptation to indulge in unwise sexual behaviour, smoking or drinking or gluttony.

Idle talk may make us lose our focus and sense of purpose, so we must avoid talkativeness. If a person we are dealing with starts indulging in idle talk, we can just listen and not say anything that would encourage him to go on. But we may need to talk to people to gather information about the problem and how we can solve it. So, we cannot avoid talking altogether.

We need to focus on the things that need to be done on that day. We cannot expect to solve your entire life's problems at one go.

So, when we face major problems, our duty is to remember the Lord and keep on trying. After making an effort, we can do total surrender to the Lord. At bedtime we can read a spiritual or philosophical book for a short time. We can get some rest so that we are ready to face our problems afresh the next day.

When major difficulties arise, remember the advice of the Gita: If you fix your mind on the Lord, control desire and anger, and keep on trying, you will overcome every obstacle by His grace.

THE END

* * * * *

www.ingramcontent.com/pod-product-compliance
Lightning Source LLC
LaVergne TN
LVHW091056150826
845673LV00002B/605

* 9 7 9 8 8 9 1 3 3 4 4 5 8 *